Wicked Chocolate

Wicked Chocolate

JANE SUTHERING

Photography by
Debbie Patterson

CONRAN OCTOPUS

To Chocolate Lovers Everywhere

Acknowledgements

I would like to say a big thank you to: my
family and friends, who have tasted more
chocolate recipes than could ever be
reasonably expected of them; Emma, my
ever-enthusiastic assistant; and Debbie,
friend first and photographer second, who
has photographed my recipes so
fantastically and then dutifully tasted
them all!

Designer Paul Welti
Art Director Mary Evans
Photographer and Stylist Debbie Patterson
Illustrator Alison Barratt
Food Stylist Jane Suthering
Project Editor Louise Simpson
Editorial Assistant Jo Mead
Production Controller Jill Macey
Copy Editor Lewis Esson

A CIP record for this book is available from the British Library

ISBN 1 85029 447 X

Typeset by Servis Filmsetting Ltd, Manchester.

Printed in Hong Kong

First published in 1992 by
Conran Octopus Limited
37 Shelton Street, London WC2H 9HN

Text Copyright © Jane Suthering 1992
Photography copyright © Debbie Patterson 1992
Design and layout copyright © Conran Octopus

Contents

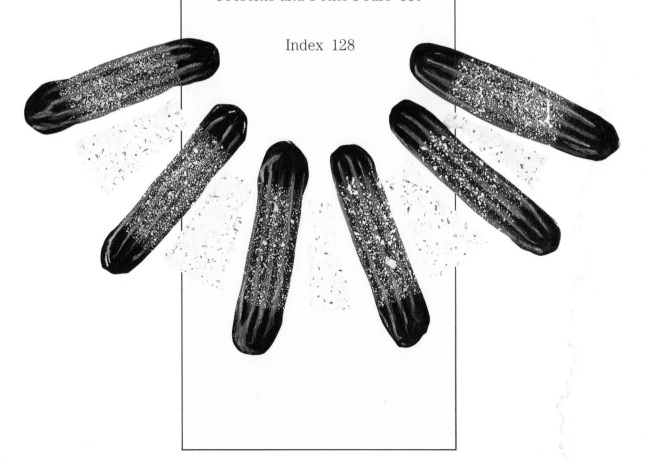

Introduction

*As some people say that chocolate is a
more reliable source of pleasure than
romance, it obviously needs to be taken
seriously. Getting to know the different
types of chocolate, choosing your
favourites and learning to work with
them successfully is the first step.*

Chocolate Cravings

No wonder we think of chocolate as wicked – whether it's eaten purely for pleasure or secretly indulged in – this beguiling comfort food has a lot to answer for.

What is it about the stuff that has inspired us to discuss it, argue and become authoritative about it, arrange parties, holiday weekends and cookery courses around it, introduce words like 'chocophile' and 'chocaholic' into our language and even create The Chocolate Society?

Rich and luscious, delectable and moreish, it's one of the foods we most crave – although there's great controversy about whether we can actually become addicted to it – so much so that we manage to eat our way through billions of pounds each year (something like 7–9kg/15–20lb per person!).

Somebody must be helping me out with my quota! I have bars of chocolate sitting in the fridge or pantry for weeks and never touch them, then suddenly I really do crave for some.

When? When I'm setting off on a long journey I invariably buy a bar to keep me going; when I'm rushing round shopping all day and know I haven't got time to stop for lunch; and when it comes to the end of yet another hectic day and I'm drinking a black coffee after an evening meal – you guessed it, all I want is one tiny morsel of chocolate!

So you can imagine, I've been having something of a love–hate relationship with chocolate over the last few months as I've been writing this book. While experimenting with one sweet chocolate recipe after another, I've often yearned for something simple and savoury such as a cheese and pickle sandwich. On the other hand, there have been times when eating the first course of a meal, I've hardly been able to contain my excitement waiting for the last course so that I could taste my latest sweet concoction!

Chocolate has certainly got its hooks into me. Whatever your feelings about chocolate, I hope *Wicked Chocolate* gives you some of the pleasure that writing it has given me.

*Previous pages
A selection of chocolate decorations, including Chocolate Leaves, Butterflies, Curls, Shavings, Shapes and Scribbles*

The History of Chocolate

Cocoa trees (*Theobroma Cacao*– 'Theobroma' meaning 'food of the gods') have grown in Central America for over four thouand years and it is the beans of the cocoa tree that are used to make chocolate.

Originally, chocolate was only made for drinking. It wasn't until the nineteenth century that it was produced as edible blocks.

The Aztec God Quetzalcoatl is said to have been the first to teach his people how to make chocolate from the beans of the wild cocoa tree. The seeds were then spread throughout Central America by monkeys, birds and man. The Mayan Indians – originally from Guatemala – established some of the first cocoa plantations in the Yucatan around AD 600, when cocoa was considered so important the beans were used as a currency.

Supposedly, Christopher Columbus tasted a chocolate drink in 1502 in Nicaragua but was far from impressed, so its introduction into Europe was left to Hernán Cortés, the great Spanish *conquistador*, who tasted chocolate in 1519 at a banquet given by Aztec Emperor Montezuma in what is now Mexico City.

Xocoatl, as it was then known, was served as a cold frothy drink that was flavoured with honey, spices and vanilla. It was highly valued even then, for the effects of its caffeine and other stimulating qualities.

It was also believed to have aphrodisiacal powers – Montezuma used to drink a golden goblet full of chocolate every time he entered his harem, to give him vigour and strength – and, he hoped, some of the wisdom of the Gods.

Mixed with sugar, chocolate soon became a favourite drink of the Spanish court and eventually the idea of drinking chocolate spread throughout Europe as fast as its high price would allow.

In 1657 the first chocolate house appeared in London and soon chocolate became very popular in Britain's major cities as a hot drink. This 'food of the gods' was considered to have great therapeutic qualities – again as an aphrodisiac, but also as a medicine or tonic:

*'Twill make old women young and
  fresh;
create new motions of the flesh,
and cause them long for you know
  what,
if they but taste of chocolate.'*

Throughout Europe, chocolate was being acclaimed a phenomenon – as one German scientist put it 'for nowhere else has nature concentrated such a wealth of valuable nourishment in so small a space' – and the chocolate industry began to flourish.

The pioneers of the British chocolate industry are still the leading lights of today. Fry and Sons was established in 1728, but it wasn't until 1847 that the company introduced chocolate for eating. By this time a press had been invented to extract cocoa butter from the bean, so Fry's added cocoa mass and sugar to this butter and made the first eating chocolate.

Cadbury's opened a tea and coffee shop in Birmingham and were soon serving their own chocolate drink. By 1849 they too were selling chocolate for eating.

Great developments were to follow. In Switzerland, Nestle's created milk chocolate and Lindt developed fondant chocolate, which was much smoother in texture and melted in the mouth. In Holland, Van Houten invented the process which allowed chocolate to become soluble in liquids, and firms like Menier flourished in France.

Today chocolate is big business, with individual manufacturers carefully guarding their secrets and giving us a fantastic if mind-boggling choice.

How Cocoa Trees Grow

The cocoa tree is an eccentric tree which produces leaves, flowers and fruit all at the same time. About 100,000 pink and white blossoms appear on each tree every year and the leaves vary in colour from pale green to lavender or purple, all maturing to dark green. The oval bean pods grow directly on the trunk and the thicker main branches – up to 30 at one time – ripening from green to yellow or red.

The trees are vulnerable to the elements and disease for their first 3–4 years, then they start producing fruit at about the age of 8, reaching a limit of productivity when they are between 30–40 years old.

The pods are harvested by hand twice a year. They are then broken open to reveal about 40 cocoa beans embedded in a delicious white pulp. This mass of beans and pulp is then left to ferment for several days, and the beans are turned occasionally until they are brown. The beans are then cleaned off and dried in the sun. An average tree yields 500g–1kg/1–2lb of dried beans per year.

Today, much of the world's cocoa crop comes from Brazil and West Africa. There are two main types of bean used by the chocolate industry:

The *Forastero* or *base bean*, as it is easy to grow, forms 90% of the world crop and is used to make the bulk of most finished chocolate. It has a dark purplish bean which is harsh in flavour.

Criollo is the flavour bean and is blended into every fine chocolate. It is more difficult to grow, being susceptible to disease and the vagaries of the weather. However, the yellow-white bean is finer and milder in flavour than the forastero. Some of the world's finest chocolate is supposedly made from this bean alone.

How Chocolate is Made

The cleaned, dried beans are roasted to bring out their flavour and at this stage they give off a wonderful aroma similar to roasting coffee beans. They are then cracked into pieces and the shells discarded, leaving the pieces of kernel or 'nibs'.

The nibs are ground between rollers and this extracts their fat content or 'cocoa butter', leaving a thick dark brown paste known as 'cocoa mass' or 'chocolate liquor' which hardens as it cools. Cooled and hardened – with no added ingredients except perhaps a little cocoa butter – this is sold as unsweetened baking chocolate. If the cocoa mass is then rolled further, more cocoa butter will be released and the remaining hard mass is ground to make what we know as cocoa powder.

The cocoa mass may also be blended with additional cocoa butter, sugar and flavourings, such as vanilla, to make most types of eating and cooking chocolate.

The ingredients are worked together and then further refined to give the chocolate its smooth texture. In most cases it goes through a process known as 'conching', in which it is passed between fine rollers while being heated, to give it extra smoothness. It is then tempered, by heating and cooling it and finally flavoured and shaped as required.

Types of Chocolate

Plain or dark chocolate (bitter-sweet or semi-sweet)

This includes dessert chocolate and true cooking chocolate. It must contain a minimum of 34% cocoa solids (cocoa mass and cocoa butter). The greater the percentage of cocoa solids the better the quality of chocolate, so always look at the information on the packaging. There are a lot of readily available chocolate bars with cocoa solid percentages in the high 50's, 60's and even up to the 70's. Usually, the higher the amount of cocoa solids the darker and less sweet the chocolate will be.

A dessert chocolate, such as Bournville, contains a minimum 34% cocoa solids, but for a richer taste look out for other readily available makes, such as Terry's, Bendick's, Menier and Lindt. 'Continental' chocolate, such as Waitrose's own-brand (with 72% minimum cocoa solids) or Valrohna, are worth searching for.

Unsweetened chocolate

This is not readily available in the shops and has to be specially ordered from suppliers. It is made from cocoa mass with only a little cocoa butter added. It is expensive but gives excellent results in cooking.

A reasonable substitute may be made by blending 30g/1oz cocoa powder with 15g/½oz butter for every 30g/1oz unsweetened chocolate required in a recipe.

Milk chocolate

This is made in a similar way to plain chocolate, but has less cocoa mass added. Instead milk is added either in condensed or dried form. Milk chocolate is much sweeter and milder in flavour than plain chocolate, and is generally used as an eating chocolate – although I have used it occasionally in recipes to give a contrast of colour or flavour.

White chocolate

This doesn't contain any of the cocoa mass, but is a mixture of cocoa butter with sugar, flavouring and milk added. It is used more for its novelty value and to give a contrast of colour as it doesn't have anything like the depth of flavour of dark chocolate.

The best readily available one I have found to use is Lindt, which melts easily without caking. Inferior brands use vegetable oil in place of cocoa butter, so examine the ingredients details on the packaging carefully.

Chocolate-flavoured coatings and coverings

These are usually about half the price of 'real' chocolate because they contain only about 2.5% cocoa solids and generally incorporate vegetable fat instead of cocoa butter. They don't taste nearly as nice as chocolate, but they do melt more easily and when re-set they keep a good gloss. For these reasons they are useful for making decorations such as curls and leaves – but they don't taste very nice!

To make a better 'covering chocolate', stir 1 tablespoon of vegetable oil into each 225g/8oz of good-quality melted chocolate.

Chocolate drops

These are even-sized pieces of chocolate specially designed to stay whole in baking without melting. Use them in biscuits and puddings.

Couverture

This is a confectioner's chocolate, which is difficult to get hold of except through trade suppliers, superior kitchen shops or independent chocolate shops. It needs to be 'tempered' to stabilize its high cocoa butter content. This involves heating it to 43C/110F then cooling it to 26C/80F, before heating it once more to 40C/90F before it may be used.

Diabetic chocolate

This is made in a similar way to chocolate, but the sugar is replaced by other sweeteners. Beware, however, this doesn't necessarily make it low in calories!

Carob

This is not chocolate at all, but is made from the carob bean, which doesn't taste anything like cocoa. However, it is brown and can be flavoured and treated to make a product similar to chocolate. It is popular with health-food enthusiasts and people allergic to chocolate.

On the Scientific Side of Chocolate

Arguments abound as to whether or not chocolate is addictive and if it can cause allergic reactions. Some theorize that it could be the cause of innumerable ailments – from depression and hyper-activity to ulcers and arthritis.

Whatever the answer, here are a few interesting facts to mull over, perhaps while biting into your next piece of chocolate!

- The predominant stimulant in cocoa is theobromine, which is similar to caffeine (also present in chocolate), but milder in its effect on the nervous system.

- Chocolate has considerable food value as it is packed with energy and contains some tannin, fat, starch, protein, B vitamins and mineral salts – in particular iron. Milk chocolate contains useful amounts of iron as well as calcium and vitamins A, B and D.

- Pure chocolate contains phenyl-ethylamine, a substance that produces a giddy response comparable to an amphetamine 'high'. It has even been said that the body's production of this chemical is responsible for giving people the intense feelings associated with being in love – so the joy of eating chocolate is closely akin to that of being in love. This may also explain the tradition of giving chocolates to loved ones.

- Chocolate contains tyramine – also found in red wine and a wide range of foods as diverse as pickled herrings, broad beans, yeast and meat extracts and cheese – which may cause the blood vessels in the head to constrict and so trigger headaches.

Melting Chocolate

First, always be sure to break the chocolate into even-sized pieces so that it melts smoothly.

Place the pieces of chocolate in a small bowl and put this in a metal sieve or colander set over a saucepan of simmering water – this way the bowl will not touch the water and get too hot. Warm it just until the chocolate melts, stirring occasionally with a plastic spatula or metal spoon. As soon as it is melted and smooth, remove it from the heat.

Alternatively, chocolate may be melted in the microwave on Medium. Times will vary with the amount of chocolate used and the power of the microwave. Take a look at the manufacturer's booklet before you start!

In general, chocolate being melted in the microwave should be heated in a glass or plastic bowl for 1 minute. Then check the consistency by touching it with a fingertip or a plastic spatula. (Chocolate can be deceptive as it often keeps its form even when it's almost melted.) If necessary, return it to the microwave and

cook for another 30 seconds and then test again. Do this until the chocolate is melted. Remember, however, that chocolate has a tendency to burn if not watched carefully – especially white chocolate.

I did want to provide a chart of melting times in this section, but found that experiments with different microwaves and different chocolates gave such varying results that it will have to be left to your own trial and error!

Making Chocolate Decorations

For the beginner, making chocolate decorations can be so very frustrating, but I am afraid practice is the only way to success.

Different chocolates melt in different ways, giving such varying consistencies – the cheaper cake coverings make fantastic curls but the taste is nowhere near as good as a good-quality chocolate. The latter, however, can be very brittle and may splinter as you try to scrape it off a surface to make the curls.

One saving grace is that all chocolate will pipe well once it cools and thickens to a suitable consistency.

Chocolate Shavings

Pull a potato peeler evenly across the surface of a bar of chocolate at room temperature to produce shavings. (If the chocolate is chilled, the shavings will shatter.)

Alternatively, spread melted chocolate in a thin layer on a marble or other smooth surface and leave until set. Scrape shavings from the chocolate by holding the blade of a knife at an oblique angle and pushing it across the chocolate.

Store chocolate shavings in an airtight container in the fridge.

Chocolate Shapes

Spread melted chocolate evenly on a sheet of baking parchment secured on a tray. Tap the tray firmly on a work surface to level the chocolate. Leave to cool until just set but not hard, then stamp out shapes with a cutter or cut geometric shapes with a sharp knife.

Using a palette knife, carefully transfer the shapes to a tray and leave them to set hard. Stored in an airtight container in the fridge, layered between sheets of baking parchment, they will last for a few weeks.

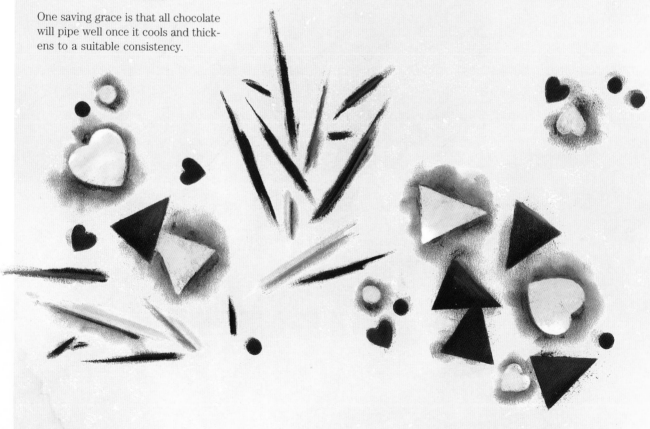

Chocolate Scribbles

Fill a small greaseproof paper piping bag with melted and cooled chocolate. Pipe formal or abstract shapes on a sheet of baking parchment secured on a tray. Leave until hard, then carefully lift the scribbles off the paper. Store in an airtight container in the fridge, layered between sheets of baking parchment.

Chocolate Butterflies

Draw the outline of a butterfly on a piece of baking parchment. Fold the paper in half down the middle of the body of the butterfly to make a crease, then open the paper out again and secure it flat on a tray. Using a greaseproof paper piping bag, pipe chocolate on the outline of the butterfly and fill in the wings with a loose zig-zag of lines. Then carefully fold the paper so the wings are at right angles (support them in the corner of a large tin or on a shelf) and leave until set. Carefully peel the butterfly off the paper. Store in an airtight container in the fridge.

Chocolate Leaves

Brush melted chocolate evenly all over the underside of fresh, clean, dry, non-poisonous leaves such as bay, lemon or orange, ficus (weeping fig) or rose (these all have raised veins on the underside which will give a decorative effect). Leave to set hard, then carefully peel away the leaf to leave a chocolate replica.

For ornate centrepieces, chocolate artichoke leaves or cabbage leaves may be prepared in the same way. They may then be stuck together with a little melted chocolate or Chocolate Modelling Paste (see page 19). Chocolate cabbage leaves make good containers for presenting petits fours.

Store chocolate leaves in an airtight container in the fridge, layered between sheets of baking parchment.

Chocolate Curls

Simple chocolate curls are made like Chocolate Shavings (see page 16) by first spreading the chocolate on a smooth surface. Then, when it is set but not too hard, scrape across the top with a flexible knife or new paint scraper held at an oblique angle.

Two-tone curls can be made by spreading some dark chocolate on the surface and then spreading some white chocolate next to it so that they are touching along one long edge. Allow to cool and then scrape down the join to pick up some of each colour in the curl.

Lemon Tartlets decorated with Chocolate Butterflies

Chocolate Modelling Paste

Adding a little corn syrup to plain chocolate turns it into a malleable paste which can be used as a rollable icing to cover cakes (see Chocolate Ribbon Cake on page 44) or as a mouldable container for fillings (see Chocolate Moneybags on page 121).

200g/7oz plain chocolate, broken into pieces
3 tbsp light corn syrup

Place the chocolate and syrup in a bowl set over a saucepan of simmering water and stir until the chocolate has just melted. Remove from the heat and beat until smooth. Leave the mixture to cool.

When cool enough to handle, knead to a smooth paste on a clean work surface. If at any time the paste becomes too hard, wrap it in clingfilm and warm it in the microwave for a few seconds on Low.

Chocolate Sauces

Chocolate sauces make wonderful accompaniments to many things, especially ice-cream or hot puddings – or even chocolate cakes and desserts!

Chocolate Sauce

115g/4 oz cocoa powder
225g/8oz caster sugar
55g/2oz plain chocolate, broken into even-sized pieces

Mix the cocoa powder to a paste with 200ml/7fl oz water.

In a saucepan, dissolve the caster sugar in 200ml/7fl oz water over a gentle heat.

Stir the cocoa paste into the sugar syrup and bring to the boil, stirring constantly. Remove from the heat and stir in the chocolate until melted.

Chocolate Cream Sauce

300ml/½pt double cream
140g/5oz plain or milk chocolate, broken into even-sized pieces

In a small saucepan, heat the cream to just below boiling point.

Immediately remove from the heat, add the chocolate and stir until it is melted and the mixture is smooth.

Serve at once. If the sauce should cool, warm it gently over a low heat.

Morning Munchies

In the eighteenth century every self-respecting citizen would start their day with a jug of steaming hot chocolate. What could be nicer than to revive this tradition and add a flaky chocolate pastry to the Sunday breakfast tray.

The Ultimate Hot Chocolate

This is a far cry from hot milk flavoured with drinking chocolate. As it is undeniably rich and wicked make sure you serve it in small amounts!

MAKES 4

170g/6oz plain chocolate, broken into small pieces
575ml/1pt milk
whipped cream, to serve
ground cinnamon or cocoa powder, to serve

Place the chocolate in a small saucepan with 4 tablespoons of water and heat gently until melted.

In another saucepan, bring the milk just to the boil. Add this to the melted chocolate and whisk continuously until frothy.

Serve in cups or glasses, topped with whipped cream and sprinkled with either cinnamon or cocoa powder.

Previous pages
The Ultimate Hot Chocolate and Mrs Asbeck's Stollen

Cannoli

I ate my first cannoli in a small Italian restaurant in Baltimore on a tour of the States some years ago and was determined to have a go at making them myself.

Some lengths of wooden dowelling are needed for this recipe. Go to your nearest woodyard or hardware shop and ask for twelve 15cm/6in lengths from dowelling which is 2.5cm/1in thick.

MAKES 12

140g/5oz plain flour
15g/½oz icing sugar
2 tsp cocoa powder
pinch of salt
15g/½oz butter
3 tbsp Marsala
white of 1 egg, lightly beaten
vegetable oil, for deep-frying
icing sugar, to dust
cocoa powder, to dust

FOR THE FILLING

285g/10oz Mascarpone cheese
3 tbsp chopped pistachio nuts
45g/1½oz icing sugar, sifted
45g/1½oz glacé fruits, finely chopped
45g/1½oz plain chocolate, finely chopped

Sift the flour, icing sugar, cocoa powder and salt into a bowl. Rub in the butter and mix to a firm dough with the Marsala and 2 tablespoons of water. Knead lightly, then wrap and leave to rest for 30 minutes.

On a lightly floured surface, roll the dough out thinly and stamp out twelve 10cm/4in rounds.

Lightly butter the lengths of dowelling and wrap a piece of dough around each one sealing the overlap with a little of the beaten egg white.

Heat the oil to 180C/350F (or until a small cube of dry bread browns in 60 seconds) and deep-fry the cannoli in batches, until crisp and golden. Drain on paper towels. When cool enough to handle, slide them off the wooden sticks and leave them to cool on a wire rack.

Make the filling by beating together all the ingredients. Using a piping bag fitted with a large plain nozzle, fill each cannoli with the Mascarpone mixture. Dust with icing sugar and cocoa powder and serve as fresh as possible.

Mrs Asbeck's Stollen

Mrs Asbeck is the mother of one of my closest friends from school days. It is always a delight to visit her house at Christmas, where guests are tempted by the array of German cookies and cakes she traditionally makes.

Her stollen has always been one of my favourites. With her kind permission, I have added a chocolate marzipan centre to make it even more fabulous – if that's possible!

55g/2oz fresh yeast or 30g/1oz dried yeast
250ml/8fl oz lukewarm water
115g/4oz caster sugar, plus 1 extra tablespoon, to dust
500g/1lb 2oz strong plain flour
¾ tsp salt
¼ tsp ground cardamom
¼ tsp freshly grated nutmeg
¼ tsp ground cinnamon
255g/9oz unsalted butter, diced and softened, plus more for greasing
finely grated zest of ½ a lemon
85g/3oz currants
225g/8oz sultanas
85g/3oz candied orange peel, diced
85g/3oz candied lemon peel, diced
85g/3oz flaked almonds
1 tbsp icing sugar

FOR THE MARZIPAN
115g/4oz ground almonds
115g/4oz plain chocolate, melted
30g/1oz caster sugar
white of 1 egg

Dissolve the yeast in the lukewarm water and add 1 tablespoon of the caster sugar.

Sift the flour, salt and spices into a bowl and make a well in the centre. Pour in the yeast mixture and leave in a warm place for about 20 minutes, until the yeast mixture is frothy.

Add the remaining sugar, 225g/8oz of the butter and the lemon zest and beat to a soft dough. Using a dough hook, if possible, knead well for about 10 minutes. Cover and leave to rise in a warm place for 30–45 minutes, until doubled in size.

Knead once more for about 5 minutes, then work in the fruit and nuts. Cover and leave to rise again in a warm place for 30–45 minutes, until doubled in size.

Meanwhile, make the marzipan: combine all the ingredients until smooth. Set aside.

On a lightly floured surface, knead the dough quickly. Press it out roughly to an oval shape about 40cm/16in long.

Roll the marzipan to a cylinder about 2cm/¾in thick and 30cm/12in long and place in the centre of the dough. Fold both long edges in over the marzipan and tuck the shorter ends under to enclose the marzipan completely.

Set the dough on a large baking tray which has been greased with butter. Cover and leave to rise in a warm place for about 1 hour until well risen (the dough should spring back when lightly pressed with the fingertips).

Preheat the oven to 200C/400F/gas6.

Bake the dough for 30 minutes. Reduce the oven temperature to 180C/350F/gas4 and cook the stollen for about 15–20 minutes more, until golden brown. The base of the stollen should sound hollow when tapped with the knuckles. If it is becoming too browned before it is thoroughly cooked, cover it loosely with kitchen foil.

Melt the remaining butter and brush it over the stollen whilst still warm. Sprinkle with the extra tablespoon of caster sugar, then put the icing sugar in a sieve and dredge this over the top. Allow to cool on a wire rack.

Serve cut in slices. If it ever gets the chance to become stale, it is also delicious toasted!

Traditional Chocolate Cake

Just what it says – this is a traditional chocolate victoria sandwich cake lightened with golden syrup and a little extra baking powder.

170g/6oz butter, softened, plus more for greasing
170g/6oz caster sugar
3 eggs
2 tbsp golden syrup, slightly warmed
140g/5oz self-raising flour
30g/1oz cocoa powder
¼ tsp baking powder

FOR THE ICING
85g/3oz butter, softened
140g/5oz icing sugar, sifted
85g/3oz milk chocolate, melted

Preheat the oven to 190C/375F/gas5. Grease two 20cm/8in sandwich tins with butter and line their bases with greaseproof paper.

Cream the butter and sugar together in a bowl until almost white. Beat the eggs and golden syrup together in another bowl and then beat this into the creamed mixture, adding a little at a time.

Sift the flour, cocoa powder and baking powder together and fold them into the creamed mixture. Divide this mixture between the two prepared tins and level the surface.

Bake for about 25 minutes, until well risen and just firm to the touch. Allow to cool slightly in the tins, then turn out and leave to cool completely on wire racks.

Make the icing: cream the butter and icing sugar together until light and fluffy, then stir in the chocolate. Use half of the icing to sandwich the two cakes together and spread the remaining icing on the top.

Chocolate Carousels

There is still something special about home-made biscuits, despite the array of ever-improving shop-bought ones. These wholesome oaty rounds spread with chocolate make a great mid-morning snack.

MAKES 18
115g/4oz butter, diced and softened
55g/2oz plain flour
1 tsp baking powder
115g/4oz porridge oats
85g/3oz caster sugar
55g/2oz desiccated coconut
1 egg, beaten
140g/5oz milk chocolate, melted

Preheat the oven to 180C/350F/gas4 and lightly grease 2 baking trays with butter.

Sift the flour and baking powder into a bowl then stir in the oats, sugar and coconut. Work in the butter and beaten egg to make a firm dough.

Alternatively, place all these ingredients in a food processor and pulse until the mixture comes away from the sides of the bowl.

On a lightly floured surface, roll out the mixture to a thickness of 6mm/¼in and stamp out eighteen 7.5cm/3in rounds, re-rolling trimmings as necessary.

Place on the prepared baking trays and bake for 20 minutes until golden brown. Cool on a wire rack.

Spread the flat surface of each biscuit with the melted chocolate and leave to set.

Jean-Claude's Croissant Dough

Jean-Claude is a baker in Honfleur and to my mind he makes the best croissants I have ever eaten. He has been kind enough to give me his dough recipe to make my chocolate croissant, so I've dedicated the Honfleur Hoops to him!

MAKES ABOUT 900G/2LB
500g/1lb 2oz strong plain flour
30g/1oz fresh yeast or 15g/½oz dried yeast
350ml/12fl oz lukewarm water
2 tsp salt
55g/2oz caster sugar
350g/12oz unsalted butter, softened

In a large bowl, mix one-quarter of the flour with the yeast and the luke-warm water to give a smooth paste. Cover and leave in a warm place for 1 hour.

Add all the remaining ingredients except the butter and mix to a soft dough. Using a dough hook, if poss-ible, knead the dough for 6–7 minutes until smooth and elastic.

Cover and leave to rise for 1 hour. Then chill for at least 8 hours, pre-ferably overnight.

On a lightly floured surface, roll out the dough to a thickness of about 1cm/½in and lightly mark it across into 3 equal bands. Shape the butter so that in fits in the central band of the dough, leaving a generous clean edge at the sides. Fold the top third of the dough to the centre to cover

the butter and the bottom third of the dough up to the centre to make a neat shape. Press the edges down well with a rolling pin. Roll out care-fully, making sure that the dough never breaks to reveal any butter.

Fold the top third of the dough down to cover the central portion, then fold the bottom third up to cover the central portion and roll out once more. Repeat this process twice more to distribute the butter evenly in layers throughout the dough. Wrap and chill for several hours until firm. Divide the dough into two equal portions. Use fresh or freeze and thaw as required.

Chocolate Croissants

MAKES 8
half quantity Jean-Claude's
Croissant Dough (see page 25)
225g/8oz plain chocolate, broken
into squares
butter, for greasing
beaten egg, to glaze

On a lightly floured surface, roll out the dough to make a very large round about 3mm/⅛in thick. Cut it into 8 triangular wedges.

Place one-eighth of the chocolate in a line near the base of each dough triangle, then roll each wedge towards its sharp point to encase the chocolate.

Curl the rolled wedges round so that the ends almost meet to make crescent shapes.

Place the croissants on baking trays which have been greased with butter. Cover and leave to rise in a warm place for about 2 hours, until the dough springs back when pressed lightly with the fingertips.

Preheat the oven to 200C/400F/gas6.

Brush the croissants with beaten egg and bake for 20–25 minutes, until crisp and golden brown. Serve as soon as possible after they come out of the oven.

Previous pages
Chocolate Croissants and Honfleur
Hoops

Honfleur Hoops

MAKES 12
115g/4oz caster sugar
115g/4oz ground almonds
55g/2oz butter, softened, plus
more for greasing
2 egg yolks
55g/2oz plain chocolate, grated
55g/2oz sultanas
2 tbsp dark rum
half quantity Jean-Claude's
Croissant Dough (see page 25)
beaten egg, to glaze

Beat together the sugar, almonds, butter, egg yolks, chocolate, sultanas and rum. Chill until required.

On a lightly floured surface, roll out the croissant dough to a 45×20cm/18×8in rectangle. Spread the chilled filling evenly over the dough, ensuring that it reaches the long sides but leaving a 2.5cm/1in clean edge along both short sides.

Starting at a short side, roll up the dough like a Swiss roll. Cut this into 12 slices and place these on baking trays which have been greased with butter. Cover and leave to rise in a warm place for about 1 hour, until the dough springs back when pressed lightly with the fingertips.

Preheat the oven to 200C/400F/gas6.

Brush the hoops with beaten egg and bake for 20–25 minutes, until crisp and golden. Serve freshly baked from the oven.

Chocrocks

Rock buns must be one of the first things I ever learned to cook, yet I stil think they are delicious. They are very definitely best eaten fresh. However, the apple in this version does mean that they will keep moist for an extra 24 hours. In the unlikely event that they last that long, refresh them in the oven!

MAKES 8

85g/3oz butter, diced and softened, plus more for greasing
100g/3½oz plain flour
2 tsp baking powder
pinch of salt
100g/3½oz wholemeal flour
85g/3oz Demerara sugar
225g/8oz dessert apple, peeled, cored and roughly chopped
55g/2oz chocolate, chopped, or chocolate drops
1 egg
2 tbsp milk

Preheat the oven to 200C/400F/gas6 and grease a baking tray with some butter.

Sift the flour, baking powder and salt into a bowl then stir in the wholemeal flour. Rub in the butter until the mixture resembles fine crumbs, then stir in the sugar, apple and chocolate.

Whisk the egg and milk together and add this to the rubbed-in mixture. Mix quickly to a stiff dough.

Divide the mixture into 8 and place them in rough mounds on the baking tray.

Bake for 15–20 minutes, until golden and just firm to the touch. Allow to cool on a wire rack.

Chocolate and Coconut Shortbread Fingers

This is an interesting variation on the well-loved caramel or million-aire's shortbread with coconut added to the caramel layer. Swirling two types of chocolate on the top gives it a decorative finish.

MAKES 20

170g/6oz plain flour
170g/6oz butter, diced
55g/2oz caster sugar
55g/2oz light Muscovado sugar
400g/14oz can of condensed milk
1 tsp lemon juice
55g/2oz desiccated coconut
140g/5oz plain or milk chocolate, melted
85g/3oz white chocolate, melted

Preheat the oven to 160C/325F/gas3.

Sift the flour into a bowl. Dice two-thirds of the butter and rub it into the flour until the mixture resembles fine crumbs. Stir in the caster sugar and press the mixture into a 28×18cm/11×7in shallow tin. Bake for 30 minutes until golden brown. Leave to cool.

Put the remaining butter, Muscovado sugar, condensed milk and lemon juice into a saucepan. Cook over a gentle heat for 15–20 minutes, stirring until the mixture is thickened and light caramel in colour. Stir in the coconut and spread this over the shortbread. Leave to cool.

Spread the darker chocolate on top of the caramel then drizzle the white chocolate on top of that. Using a skewer, swirl the surface to give a marbled effect. Leave to set, then serve cut in fingers.

Hubble-Bubble Bars

These brightly coloured bars are great fun for both adults and children.

MAKES 15
115g/4oz softened butter or soft tub margarine, plus more for greasing
115g/4oz caster sugar
2 eggs
100g/3½oz self-raising flour, sifted
15g/½oz cocoa powder, sifted
170g/6oz macadamia nuts, roughly chopped
85g/3oz marshmallows, chopped
115g/4oz Smarties

Preheat the oven to 190C/375F/gas5. Grease a 28×18cm/11×7in shallow cake tin with butter and line with greaseproof paper.

Cream the butter and sugar together until pale and fluffy. Beat in the eggs, one at a time. Fold in the flour and cocoa powder, until evenly mixed. Then stir in about one-third of the chopped nuts.

Spread the mixture in the prepared tin and bake for 15 minutes, until risen and just firm to the touch.

Sprinkle the remaining ingredients evenly on the surface of the cake and return it to the oven for 5–10 minutes, until the marshmallows have melted.

Leave to cool in the tin, then cut into bars to serve.

Flapjacks

Crisp, buttery biscuits with a hint of ginger and chocolate make a great snack. They will store well in an air-tight container.

MAKES 10
85g/3oz butter, plus more for greasing
85g/3oz Demerara sugar
115g/4oz oat flakes with bran
30g/1oz crystallized ginger, chopped
30g/1oz Brazil nuts, chopped
55g/2oz chocolate drops
55g/2oz plain or milk chocolate, melted

Preheat the oven to 200C/400F/gas6 and lightly grease a 19cm/7½in square shallow cake tin with butter.

Melt the butter in a saucepan over a gentle heat and stir in the sugar and oat flakes, followed by the ginger and nuts. Finally stir in the chocolate drops. Press the mixture into the prepared tin.

Bake for 20 minutes until golden.

While still warm from the oven, mark it into 10 bars with a sharp knife. Leave to cool and harden in the tin.

Fill a small greaseproof paper piping bag with the melted chocolate and pipe zig-zags on each piece. Leave to set before serving.

Chocolate Granola

This crunchy breakfast cereal is a great way to start the day. Make it in batches and store in an airtight container. Serve with milk, or natural yogurt and fresh fruit if you prefer.

MAKES ABOUT 900G/2LB

400g/14oz porridge oats
115g/4oz oat bran and oat germ
115g/4oz light Muscovado sugar
115g/4oz assorted nuts, chopped
55g/2oz desiccated coconut
85g/3oz sunflower seeds
30g/1oz sesame seeds
150ml/¼pt vegetable oil
2 tbsp cocoa powder, sifted
½ tsp natural vanilla essence
¼ tsp salt
115–225g/4–8oz chocolate,
chopped
milk or yogurt, to serve
fresh fruit, to serve (optional)

Preheat the oven to 200C/400F/gas6.

In a large bowl, combine the oats, oat bran and oat germ, sugar, nuts and seeds.

In another bowl, whisk together the oil, 150ml/¼pt of water, the cocoa powder, vanilla essence and salt until well combined. Stir this into the dry ingredients in the other bowl and mix thoroughly.

Transfer the mixture to 2 large baking trays and spread out evenly. Bake for 15 minutes, then stir and turn the mixture thoroughly on the trays and return to the oven for a further 15 minutes.

Allow to cool on the trays, then mix in the chopped chocolate. Store in an airtight container.

Serve with milk or yogurt and prepared fresh fruit, such as raspberries, blueberries, bananas or strawberries, if wished.

Chocolate Granola and Chocolate Panettone

Chocolate Panettone

Panettone is sold in elaborate boxes in Italian delicatessens at very high prices, yet it's simply an enriched fruit bread that you can easily make for a fraction of the cost. Mine uses some cocoa powder with the flour to make a chocolate bread base.

30g/1oz fresh yeast or 15g/½oz
dried yeast
375g/13oz strong plain flour,
sifted
150ml/¼pt lukewarm water
3 egg yolks, beaten
55g/2oz caster sugar
1 tsp salt
30g/1oz cocoa powder, sifted
140g/5oz butter, softened, plus
more for greasing
170g/6oz mixed dried fruit
55g/2oz flaked almonds, toasted
icing sugar, to dust
butter or Mascarpone cheese and
honey, to serve

Sprinkle the yeast and 2 tablespoons of the flour into the lukewarm water and leave in a warm place for about 20 minutes, until frothing well.

Add the yeast mixture to the egg yolks with the sugar and salt. Beat in the remaining flour and cocoa powder. Beat in 115g/4oz of the butter and knead with a dough hook, if possible, for 10 minutes until the dough is smooth and elastic.

Cover and leave in a warm place for about 1 hour, until doubled in size.

Knead in the fruit and nuts. Grease a 20–22cm/8–8½in round cake tin generously with butter and transfer the dough to it. Cover and leave in a warm place for ¾–1 hour, or until the mixture reaches the top of the tin.

Preheat the oven to 200C/400F/gas6.

Melt the remaining butter and brush the surface of the dough with it. Bake for 20 minutes, then brush again with butter. Reduce the oven temperature to 180C/350F/gas4 and bake for a further 30 minutes. Take out and brush with the remaining butter, then return to the oven for a further 10–15 minutes.

Unmould the bread on a wire rack and leave to cool. Dust with icing sugar and serve in slices, spread with either butter or Mascarpone cheese sweetened with honey. If the panettone should become at all stale, it is also delicious toasted.

Brownies

Choose a good-quality chocolate for this to give the best results. Brownies should always be moist and slightly gooey in the centre.

MAKES 9

140g/5oz plain chocolate, broken
into pieces
115g/4oz butter, diced, plus more
for greasing
140g/5oz light Muscovado sugar
1 tsp natural vanilla essence
2 eggs, beaten
115g/4oz self-raising flour
pinch of salt
55g/2oz Brazil nuts, chopped

Preheat the oven to 160C/325F/gas3. Grease a 20cm/8in square cake tin with butter and line the base with greaseproof paper.

Put the chocolate pieces in a saucepan with the butter and 2 tablespoons of water. Heat gently, stirring occasionally, until melted. Leave to cool slightly then stir in the sugar and vanilla, followed by the beaten eggs.

Sift the flour and salt into the chocolate mixture and fold them in together with the nuts.

Transfer the mixture to the prepared tin and bake for about 25 minutes, until well risen and just firm to the touch (it should still be slightly gooey in the centre). Leave to cool in the tin.

Cut into squares to serve.

Milk Chocolate Refrigerator Cake

This must be one of the simplest recipes in the book; quick to make but nevertheless delicious to have in the fridge to serve to unexpected guests or simply to pick at yourself!

225g/8oz milk chocolate, broken
into pieces
225g/8oz butter
2 eggs, beaten
225g/8oz plain sweet biscuits,
such as digestives or Nice,
coarsely broken
115g/4oz glacé fruits, chopped
55g/2oz walnuts or toasted
almonds, chopped

Line a 450g/1lb loaf tin with foil.

Put the chocolate pieces in a large bowl with the butter. Set over a saucepan of simmering water and stir until melted. Remove from the heat and beat the eggs into the mixture.

Stir the broken biscuits, fruit and nuts into the chocolate mixture until thoroughly incorporated.

Transfer to the prepared tin and level the surface. Chill for about 8 hours until firm. Unmould and serve cut in very thin slices.

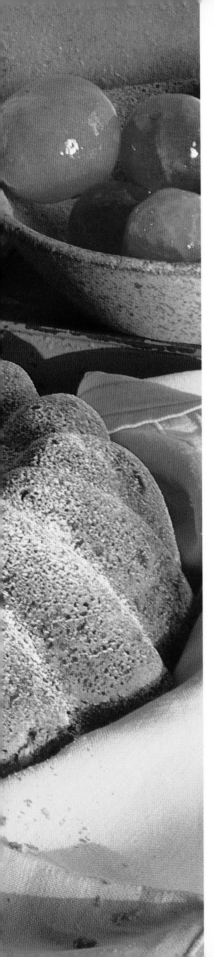

Chocolate and Orange Marble Cake

A lovely moist marbled cake that keeps beautifully in an airtight container, ready to 'cut and come again'.

250g/8½oz butter, softened
250g/8½oz golden caster sugar, plus more for sprinkling
4 large eggs, beaten
250g/8½oz self-raising flour, sifted
finely grated zest of 1 orange
55g/2oz cut mixed peel
2 tbsp orange juice or 1 tbsp orange liqueur and 1 tbsp dark rum
2 tbsp cocoa powder, sifted
85g/3oz plain chocolate, coarsely chopped
melted butter, for greasing
icing sugar, to dust

Preheat the oven to 180C/350F/gas4.

Thoroughly brush the inside of a 23cm/9in diameter (1.75l/3pt capacity) kugelhopf tin with melted butter. Then sprinkle the buttered interior with caster sugar until evenly coated. Shake out any excess.

In a large bowl, cream the butter and sugar until the mixture has a soft dropping consistency then beat in the eggs, a little at a time, until thoroughly incorporated. Fold in the sifted flour and divide the mixture into 2 equal parts.

Add the orange zest, mixed peel and half the juice or orange liqueur to one half of the butter mixture. Mix the remaining juice or rum with the cocoa until smooth, then stir this into the other half of the butter mixture together with the chopped chocolate.

Drop alternate spoonfuls of the mixtures into the prepared tin until all the mixture is used. Tap the tin sharply on the work surface to level the top. Bake for about 1 hour, until well risen and firm to the touch.

Leave the cake to cool until the tin can be handled comfortably, then shake the tin to loosen the cake. Unmould it on a wire rack, then replace the tin on top and leave until completely cold. Store in an airtight container or wrap in foil to prevent it from drying out.

Dust with icing sugar and serve, cut into slices.

Chocolate and Orange Marble Cake

Chocolate and Blueberry Muffins

These American-style muffins are best served warm straight from the oven – they're delicious as they are but even better with a knob of butter! They also freeze well.

MAKES 9

30g/1oz butter, plus more for greasing
115g/4oz wholemeal flour
115g/4oz plain flour, sifted
½ tsp baking powder
large pinch of salt
30g/1oz muscovado sugar
55g/2oz white chocolate drops
85g/3oz blueberries, fresh or frozen
150ml/¼pt milk
1 tbsp honey
½ tsp bicarbonate of soda

Preheat the oven to 200C/400F/gas6 and grease 9 muffin tins with butter or line them with large paper cases.

Mix the flours, baking powder, salt and sugar in a large bowl. Rub in the butter, then stir in the chocolate drops and blueberries.

In a small pan, warm the milk and honey together just until the honey dissolves. Stir in the bicarbonate of soda. Add to the mixture in the bowl and mix quickly.

Spoon into the prepared tins and bake for about 20 minutes, until well risen and just firm to the touch.

Unmould and allow to cool slightly. Serve as soon as possible, spread with butter if wished.

Note: try using 115g/4oz fresh cherries, stoned and quartered, instead of the blueberries.

Double Chip Cookies

There are lots of recipes for chocolate chip cookies but these are particularly good as they use two types of chocolate and whole hazelnuts to add to their chunky texture.

MAKES ABOUT 25

115g/4oz butter, softened
55g/2oz caster sugar
55g/2oz light Muscovado sugar
1 egg
½ tsp natural vanilla essence
115g/4oz plain flour
½ tsp bicarbonate of soda
½ tsp salt
45g/1½oz white chocolate, coarsely chopped
45g/1½oz plain or milk chocolate, coarsely chopped
55g/2oz roasted whole hazelnuts

Preheat the oven to 190C/375F/gas5 and grease 2 baking trays.

In a large bowl, cream the butter with the sugars until the mixture has a soft dropping consistency. Beat in the egg and vanilla essence, until well incorporated.

Sift the flour, bicarbonate of soda and salt together into the bowl and fold them in. Stir in the chopped chocolate and hazelnuts.

Drop spoonfuls of the mixture well apart on the baking trays and bake for about 12 minutes, until golden.

Allow to cool slightly then transfer to cooling racks until completely cold and store in an airtight container.

Double Chip Cookies and Chocolate and Blueberry Muffins

Teatime Treats

Whether tea is an impressive extravaganza with Opera Slices and Gâteau Lyonnais, or an essential stop-gap of Chocolate Scones and Mint Fingers for hungry kids, here are some delicious confections that will make you instantly abandon any higher thoughts of bread and butter.

White Chocolate and Strawberry Mousse Gâteau

There's a lot of effort involved in making this gâteau but the results are spectacular. Good-quality chocolate is essential to make the outer coating. I find Lindt the best to date as it melts well and spreads easily.

4 eggs
115g/4oz caster sugar
85g/3oz plain flour, sifted
30g/1oz cornflour, sifted
4 tbsp strawberry liqueur
butter, for greasing

FOR THE FILLING
450g/1lb strawberries, hulled
170g/6oz white chocolate, melted
200g/7oz fromage frais
1 tbsp gelatine dissolved in 3 tbsp water
whites of 2 eggs
30g/1oz caster sugar

TO DECORATE
350g/12oz white chocolate, melted
300ml/½pt whipping cream, whipped to soft peaks
10–12 whole strawberries

Preheat the oven to 190C/375F/gas5. Grease two 24cm/9½in cake tins with butter and line their bases with some greaseproof paper.

Previous pages
Chocolate Ribbon Cake, White Chocolate Cheesecake and White Chocolate and Strawberry Mousse Gâteau

Whisk the eggs and sugar in a large bowl set over simmering water until thick and foamy – the whisk should leave a thick trail in the mixture. Fold in the flour and cornflour and divide the mixture between the tins.

Level the surface and bake for 12–15 minutes until well risen, golden and just firm to the touch. Cool in the tins, then unmould on wire trays.

Make the filling: purée half the strawberries and quarter or halve the remainder. Sieve the purée.

Beat together the white chocolate and fromage frais. Stir a little of the strawberry purée into the gelatine and water mixture, then return that to the bulk of the purée. Fold this into the white chocolate mixture.

Whisk the egg whites until they are stiff and then whisk in the sugar. Fold this into the strawberry mixture, then fold in the chopped strawberries.

To assemble the gâteau: line the sides of a 24cm/9½in springform tin with baking parchment. Place one layer of sponge in it and sprinkle this with half the strawberry liqueur.

Pour in the strawberry mixture and top with the second sponge. Sprinkle with remaining strawberry liqueur. Press down lightly and chill for at least 4 hours, or preferably overnight. Unmould on a flat plate.

To decorate the gâteau: cut a strip of double thickness baking parchment to fit exactly around the cake and stand about 1cm/½in higher than its top. Spread this evenly with the cooled chocolate and then carefully wrap it around the cake. Chill in the freezer for 15 minutes.

Carefully peel away the paper, leaving a hard chocolate layer around the cake. Fill the centre with whipped cream and decorate with the strawberries.

White Chocolate Cheesecake

The secret of a good baked cheese-cake is not to overcook it, so this white chocolate one is left in the oven to set in the fading heat.

FOR THE BASE
225g/8oz digestible biscuits, crushed
100g/3½oz butter, melted
2 tbsp cocoa powder, sifted
2 tbsp light Muscovado sugar

FOR THE FILLING
170g/6oz white chocolate, broken into pieces
175ml/6fl oz whipping cream
450g/1lb curd cheese
115g/4oz caster sugar
1 tbsp plain flour
4 eggs
1 tsp natural vanilla essence

FOR THE TOPPING
300ml/½pt soured cream
2 tbsp caster sugar
1 tbsp cocoa powder, sifted

Preheat the oven to 190C/375F/gas5.

Combine the ingredients for the base and press the mixture into the bottom and about 2.5cm/1in up the sides of a 24cm/9½in springform tin. Bake for 10 minutes, then leave to cool slightly.

Make the filling: melt the chocolate with half the cream, either in a microwave or in a bowl set over a saucepan of simmering water, and mix until smooth.

In a bowl, beat together the remaining cream, cheese, sugar, flour, eggs and vanilla essence. Stir in the chocolate mixture and pour into the biscuit case. Bake for another 45 minutes, until almost set and lightly golden at the edges.

Make the topping: mix the soured cream and sugar in a bowl, then pour off about one-sixth of the mixture into another bowl and beat the cocoa powder into it.

Carefully spoon the plain white mixture on top of the cheesecake, then drizzle the cocoa-flavoured mixture on top to give a decorative effect.

Return to the oven for 5 minutes, then switch off the heat and leave the cake to cool completely in the oven. When completely cool, transfer to the refrigerator to chill.

Remove the cake from the tin and serve cut in thin wedges.

Chocolate Ribbon Cake

This cake is wrapped like a present to give it a spectacular finish, so decorate it when you have plenty of time to spend on the finishing touches.

55g/2oz currants
2–3 tbsp brandy
170g/6oz butter, diced, plus more
for greasing
200g/7oz plain chocolate, broken
into pieces
2 tbsp very strong black coffee
140g/5oz caster sugar, plus more
for sprinkling
5 eggs, separated
85g/3oz self-raising flour, sifted
pinch of salt

TO DECORATE
3 tbsp apricot jam, warmed and
sieved
400g/14oz white almond paste
1 quantity Chocolate Modelling
Paste (see page 19)
icing sugar, for sprinkling

Soak the currants in brandy for at least 1 hour, or up to 24 hours, in a warm place.

Preheat the oven to 160C/325F/gas3. Grease a 22cm/8½in cake tin with butter and line the base with grease-proof paper.

Melt the chocolate with the coffee, either in a bain marie or directly over the heat, stirring until smooth. Stir in about two-thirds of the sugar and all the butter and stir until melted. Remove from the heat.

Beat in the egg yolks and then stir in the flour until evenly combined. Drain the currants and stir them into the mixture.

Whisk the egg whites with a pinch of salt until stiff. Then whisk in the remaining sugar until glossy. Fold into the chocolate mixture and transfer to the prepared tin.

Bake for 45–50 minutes, until well risen and just firm to the touch. Allow to cool in the tin. As soon as the tin is cool enough to handle, unmould the cake on a wire rack and leave to cool completely.

To decorate: brush the surface of the cake with apricot jam. On a lightly sugared surface, roll out a generous half of the almond paste and use it to cover the cake. Neaten the edges and reserve the trimmings.

Warm the chocolate modelling paste (15–20 seconds in the microwave on Medium), then roll out a generous three-quarters on a surface which has been lightly sprinkled with icing sugar. Use to cover the cake, reserving the trimmings.

Roll out the reserved almond paste trimmings and make 8 long ribbons about 2cm/¾in wide to go across the cake. Re-roll the trimmings to make 8 short ribbons and a loop about the same width to make a 'bow'.

Roll out the chocolate trimmings and make the same number of ribbons but about 6mm/¼in wide.

Press a chocolate ribbon on each almond paste ribbon. Attach the ribbons to the cake to make it look like a wrapped present.

Chocolate Ribbon Cake

Chocolate and Date Squares

The combination of orange juice and dates keeps these squares nice and moist.

MAKES 24

*115g/4oz butter, softened, plus
more for greasing
255g/9oz stoned dates
125ml/4fl oz orange juice
170g/6oz plain chocolate, chopped
115g/4oz light Muscovado sugar
2 eggs
170g/6oz self-raising flour, sifted
115g/4oz walnut pieces, roughly
chopped
1–2 tbsp milk*

FOR THE TOPPING

*115g/4oz plain chocolate, chopped
115g/4oz Greek or thick-set
natural yogurt
24 toasted walnut halves*

Preheat the oven to 190C/375F/gas5. Grease a Swiss roll tin with butter and line the base with greaseproof paper.

Place the dates, 125ml/4fl oz of water and the orange juice in a small saucepan and bring just to the boil. Simmer for about 5 minutes, until the dates are soft. Stir in the chocolate until melted.

Cream the butter and sugar until pale and fluffy, then beat in the eggs one at a time.

Fold in the flour followed by the chocolate and date mixture and the walnuts until all are evenly combined. Add a little milk, if necessary, to give a dropping consistency.

Spread the mixture evenly in the prepared tin and bake for about 20 minutes, until well risen and firm to the touch. Leave to cool in the tin.

Make the topping: melt the chocolate in a small bowl set over simmering water, then remove it from the heat and allow to cool. Stir in the yogurt until thoroughly combined.

Spread the mixture on top of the baked layer. Mark in squares and place a walnut half in the centre of each square.

Serve, cut as required, and store any not eaten immediately in an airtight container in a cool place.

Opera Slices

This is my version of a classic gâteau, usually decorated with 'Opera' written in chocolate on the top. However it is made, the combination of chocolate and coffee is delightful.

MAKES 12

FOR THE SPONGE
3 eggs
85g/3oz caster sugar
85g/3oz plain flour, sifted
3 tbsp dark rum

FOR THE CHOCOLATE FILLING
115g/4oz plain chocolate, broken into pieces
125ml/4fl oz double cream
15g/½oz butter

FOR THE COFFEE FILLING
1 tbsp instant coffee
2 tsp boiling water
2 tbsp icing sugar, sifted
300ml/½pt double cream, whipped to stiff peaks

FOR THE CHOCOLATE ICING
55g/2oz plain chocolate, broken into pieces
25g/¾oz unsalted butter

Preheat the oven to 220C/425F/gas7 and line a Swiss roll tin with baking parchment.

First make the sponge: whisk the eggs and sugar in a bowl set over a saucepan of simmering water until thick and pale. The whisk should leave a strong trail in the mixture. Remove from the heat and fold in the flour.

Transfer the mixture to the prepared tin and level the surface. Bake for 8–10 minutes until just set and golden. Leave to cool in the tin and then turn out on a flat surface.

Trim the edges and cut the oblong into 3 equal strips. Drizzle each piece with 1 tablespoon of rum.

Make the chocolate filling: place the chocolate and cream in a small saucepan and heat gently until melted. Remove from the heat, stir in the butter then chill until spreadable.

Make the coffee filling: dissolve the coffee in the boiling water and sweeten with the sugar. Leave to go cold, then fold in the whipped cream. Chill until required.

Sandwich the sponge layers together with one layer of chocolate filling and one layer of coffee filling.

Make the icing: melt the chocolate and butter together in a small pan. Allow to cool slightly, then spread smoothly over the top of the sponge. Chill until firm.

Serve cut in slices.

Mint Fingers

The idea for these comes from a traditional Yorkshire recipe – all I've done is add chocolate, which combines so well with mint.

FOR THE PASTRY
225g/8oz plain flour
generous pinch of salt
85g/3oz butter or half butter and
half white fat at room
temperature, diced
beaten egg, to glaze
1 tbsp granulated sugar, to glaze

FOR THE FILLING
55g/2oz butter, softened
55g/2oz caster sugar
85g/3oz currants
55g/2oz plain or milk chocolate,
chopped, or chocolate drops
3 tbsp chopped fresh mint

Preheat the oven to 220C/425F/gas7.

First make the pastry: sift the flour and salt into a bowl and rub in the butter until the mixture resembles fine crumbs. Stir in sufficient cold water (3–4 tablespoons) to give a firm dough.

On a lightly floured surface, roll out a generous half of the pastry and use it to line the base and about 1cm/½in up the sides of a 20cm/8in shallow square cake tin.

Make the filling: cream the butter and sugar together until pale then mix in the remaining ingredients. Spread the filling over the pastry base and fold down the edges. Brush lightly with water or beaten egg.

Roll out the remaining pastry and cut out a 20cm/8in square. Set it on top of the filling and press down well to seal the edges. Prick over the surface with a fork and brush with beaten egg. Sprinkle with the granulated sugar and bake for 20 minutes, until crisp and golden.

Allow to cool in the tin. Cut in half and then cut each half into 5 fingers to serve.

Bakewell Bars

A new twist to a traditional favourite – these bars are great with a relaxing cup of tea.

MAKES 20

FOR THE PASTRY
170g/6oz plain flour
2½ tbsp cocoa powder
pinch of salt
125g/4½oz unsalted butter
2 tbsp caster sugar

FOR THE FILLING
85g/3oz butter at room
temperature
85g/3oz caster sugar
1 egg
30g/1oz plain flour, sifted
45g/1½oz chocolate cake crumbs
85g/3oz ground almonds
2 tbsp milk
4 tbsp raspberry or apricot jam
30g/1oz flaked almonds (optional)

Preheat the oven to 190C/375F/gas5.

Make the pastry: sift the flour, cocoa powder and salt into a bowl. Rub in the butter until the mixture resembles fine crumbs. Then stir in the sugar and mix to a firm dough with 1½ tablespoons of cold water.

Alternatively, pulse all these ingredients in a food processor until the dough leaves the sides of the bowl.

Roll the pastry out on a lightly floured surface and use it to line a 28×18cm/11×7in shallow cake tin.

Make the filling: cream the butter and sugar until light and fluffy. Beat in the egg and then fold in the flour, crumbs and almonds. Mix to a soft dropping consistency with the milk.

Spread the jam over the pastry and top with the cake mixture. Level the surface and sprinkle lightly with flaked almonds, if using.

Bake for about 25 minutes, until well risen and just firm to the touch. Leave to cool in the tin, then cut into bars to serve.

Chocolate Nut Torte

Ground nuts give sponge cakes a moist texture and delicious flavour. Here they are sandwiched together with a rich chocolate cream and decorated with chocolate curls to give an effective finish.

5 eggs, separated
170g/6oz caster sugar
1 tbsp instant coffee granules dissolved in 1 tbsp hot water
140g/5oz ground nuts of your choice
30g/1oz fine dry breadcrumbs
1 tbsp cocoa powder, sifted
butter, for greasing
Chocolate Curls (see page 19), to decorate

FOR THE CHOCOLATE CREAM
250ml/8fl oz double cream
225g/8oz plain chocolate, broken into pieces

Preheat the oven to 190C/375F/gas5. Grease two 23cm/9in cake tins with butter and line their bases with some greaseproof paper.

Whisk the egg whites until stiff then whisk in a scant half of the sugar, a little at a time, until the mixture is thick and glossy.

Whisk the egg yolks with the remaining sugar and coffee mixture until thick and pale.

Fold the egg yolk mixture into the egg whites then fold in the nuts, crumbs and cocoa powder.

Transfer the mixture to the prepared tins, level the surfaces and bake for about 20 minutes, until well risen and just firm to the touch. Allow to cool slightly in the tins, then transfer to wire racks and leave to cool completely.

Make the chocolate cream: heat the cream and chocolate together until the chocolate is just melted. Beat until smooth, then chill until firm. Beat once more until smooth and spreadable.

Sandwich the cakes together with a little of the chocolate cream, then spread the remaining cream over the top and sides of the cake to cover it completely.

Set some Chocolate Curls on top of the cake to decorate.

Chocolate Pithiviers

To my mind, puff pastry desserts should always be served just warm, fresh from the oven and this pastry is no exception.

SERVES 6–8
115g/4oz caster sugar
115g/4oz ground almonds
55g/2oz butter, softened, plus
more for greasing
1 egg, separated, plus 1 extra yolk
2 tbsp dark rum
115g/4oz plain or milk chocolate,
melted and cooled
350g/12oz puff pastry
15g/½oz icing sugar

Combine the caster sugar, ground almonds, butter, egg yolks and rum in a bowl and beat until smooth. Stir in the chocolate and chill until required.

Cut the pastry in half and roll both pieces out on a floured surface. Cut a 23cm/9in round from each piece.

Place one round on a baking tray which has been greased with butter. Spread the filling to within 2cm/¾in of the edge and brush the edge of the pastry with water.

Mark 8 crescent-shaped evenly spaced slashes around the second round, radiating 2.5cm/1in from the centre to within 2.5cm/1in of the edge. Place this piece over the filling and seal the edges well, making a decorative edge. Chill for 30 minutes.

Preheat the oven to 200C/400F/gas6.

Mix the egg white with the icing sugar, brush the pastry lightly and bake for 20 minutes. Increase the oven heat to maximum, brush the pastry again with the egg white mixture and cook for up to 5 minutes until well glazed.

Allow to cool on a wire tray. Serve as fresh as possible, cut into wedges.

Chocolate Pivithiers and Chocolate
and Whisky Fruit Loaf

Chocolate and Whisky Fruit Loaf

In this simple recipe, the whisky gives the loaf a special kick and also helps to keep it moist. Wrap it in kitchen foil to keep, and serve it in slices with butter.

200g/7oz mixed dried fruit
300ml/½pt freshly brewed tea
255g/9oz light Muscovado sugar
350g/12oz self-raising flour, sifted
55g/2oz cocoa powder, sifted
1 tsp ground mixed spice
1 egg
4 tbsp whisky

Soak the fruit in the freshly made tea for at least 4 hours, or overnight, until well plumped.

Preheat the oven to 160C/325F/gas3. Grease a 900g/2lb loaf tin with butter and line the base with greaseproof paper.

Place the fruit and tea in a large bowl together with the remaining ingredients and beat well until evenly combined.

Transfer to the prepared tin, level the surface and bake for about 1½ hours, until well risen and firm to the touch. Test the cake with a metal skewer inserted into its centre for a count of 10: the skewer should come out clean and piping hot to the touch.

Spike the cake all over with a skewer and carefully pour over the whisky so that it will soak into the holes.

Allow to cool slightly in the tin, then unmould on a wire rack and leave until quite cold. Serve sliced and buttered.

Chocolate Madeira Cake

Cocoa powder and ground almonds replace some of the flour in this classic cake.

*225g/8oz softened butter plus
more for greasing
225g/8oz caster sugar
4 eggs, beaten
115g/4oz self-raising flour, sifted
85g/3oz plain flour, sifted
55g/2oz ground almonds
30g/1oz cocoa powder
about 2–3 tbsp milk
1 large slice of candied citron
peel*

Preheat the oven to 160C/325F/gas3. Grease a 20cm/8in round or 18cm/7in square cake tin with butter and line with greaseproof paper.

Cream the butter and sugar until pale and fluffy. Beat in the eggs a little at a time.

Sift the flours, almonds and cocoa together and fold them into the creamed mixture. Add a little milk, if necessary, to give a soft dropping consistency.

Transfer the mixture to the prepared tin and level the surface. Position a piece of citron peel in the centre.

Bake for about 1 hour, until well risen and firm to the touch. Allow to cool slightly in the tin, then unmould on a wire rack and leave to cool completely. Invert the tin over the cake whilst cooling to keep it moist.

Chocolate Chip and Ginger Shortbread

Slow cooking is needed to achieve a crispness throughout the biscuit.

MAKES 8 PIECES
115g/4oz softened butter
55g/2oz caster sugar
170g/6oz plain flour, sifted
55g/2oz plain chocolate, coarsely chopped
30g/1oz stem ginger in syrup, drained and finely chopped
caster sugar, to dust

Preheat the oven to 160C/325F/gas3 and grease a baking tray with butter.

In a bowl, cream the butter and sugar until soft. Then add the flour, chocolate and ginger and mix together quickly with the fingertips.

Roll out the dough between 2 sheets of greaseproof paper to form a neat round about 8mm/⅓in thick.

Transfer to the prepared baking tray then crimp the edges with the fingertips and mark into 8 wedges with a sharp knife. Prick decoratively with a fork and bake for about 45 minutes until golden.

Allow to cool slightly on the tray, then sprinkle with caster sugar and transfer to a wire rack until completely cold. Break into wedges to serve.

Note: replace 30g/1oz of the flour with rice flour for a finer texture.

Chocolate Chip and Ginger Shortbread, Swiss Chocolate Sandwiches and Chocolate Scones

Chocolate Scones

By replacing some of the flour in a traditional recipe with cocoa powder, I created these chocolate scones. I'm pleased I did – they're different and delicious topped with a dollop of clotted cream and some home-made jam.

MAKES ABOUT 10
210g/7½oz self-raising flour, sifted
15g/½oz cocoa powder, sifted
¼ tsp salt
45g/1½oz butter, plus more for greasing
45g/1½oz caster sugar
55g/2oz sultanas (optional)
1 egg, beaten
about 100ml/3½fl oz milk
butter or whipped or clotted cream, to serve
jam or fruit, to serve

Preheat the oven to 230C/450F/gas8 and grease a baking tray with some butter.

Combine the flour, cocoa powder and salt in a bowl. Rub in the butter until the mixture resembles fine crumbs then stir in the sugar and sultanas, if using. Add the beaten egg and sufficient milk to give a smooth soft dough.

Roll out the dough on a lightly floured surface to a thickness of about 2cm/¾in. Stamp out as many 5 cm/2in rounds as possible. Re-roll the trimmings and cut out more rounds as before. Place them close together on the prepared baking tray.

Bake for 12–15 minutes, until well risen and firm to the touch. Allow to cool on a wire rack.

Split and serve with butter or cream and jam or, spread with clotted or whipped cream and top with a selection of prepared fruits.

Swiss Chocolate Sandwiches

I used to work with Hans, a Swiss friend who frequently amazed me by putting a bar of chocolate between two slices of bread for his lunch – it tasted delicious, so I've simply refined the idea!

MAKES 12
55g/2oz Swiss plain chocolate, broken into pieces
30g/1oz unsalted butter
6 large slices of good-quality white bread, crusts removed

Melt the chocolate in a bowl set over simmering water and then allow to cool slightly. Beat in the butter until smooth. Chill for a few minutes until spreadable.

Spread 3 slices of bread with the chocolate butter and top with the remaining 3 slices of bread. Press down lightly and cut each sandwich into 4 triangles.

Chill slightly, if wished, before serving.

Gâteau Lyonnais

The sponge layers of this gâteau are flavoured with chestnuts to give a beautifully moist texture, then sandwiched together with orange marmalade and chocolate cream.

55g/2oz butter, melted, plus more for greasing
55g/2oz plain flour, plus more for dusting
170g/6oz caster sugar, plus more for dusting
410g/14½oz can of whole cooked chestnuts (in water)
pinch of salt
4 eggs
few drops of natural vanilla essence
115g/4oz plain chocolate, broken into pieces
200ml/7fl oz double cream
4–6 tbsp orange marmalade
8–10 pieces of marron glacé

Preheat the oven to 190C/375F/gas5. Grease three 20cm/8in sandwich tins with butter and line their bases with greaseproof paper. Dust the sides with a little flour and sugar.

Thoroughly drain the chestnuts and dry them on a clean kitchen towel. Then push them through a fine sieve. Sift the flour and salt together.

Whisk the eggs with a few drops of vanilla essence and the sugar in a large bowl set over simmering water until the mixture is light and frothy and the whisk leaves a trail in the mixture. Remove from the heat.

Stir one-quarter of the egg mixture into the chestnuts until smooth, then fold this back into the bulk of the egg mixture. Fold in the flour until evenly incorporated, followed by the melted butter.

Divide the mixture between the prepared tins and bake for about 15 minutes, until risen and just firm to the touch. Allow to cool slightly in the tins, then unmould on wire racks and leave to cool completely.

In a small pan, melt the chocolate with 125ml/4fl oz of the cream over a gentle heat. Stir until smooth then chill until spreadable.

Spread a scant one-third of this mixture on one cake and top with a second cake. Spread this with marmalade and top with the final cake. Use the remaining chocolate to cover the top and sides of the cake. Mark the top in 8–10 portions with a knife.

Whip the remaining cream until stiff. Pipe a rosette of this on each marked wedge and decorate with a piece of marron glacé.

Strawberry and Banana Linzertorte

A spicy chocolate pastry encases a filling of fresh strawberries and banana – a combination that was a childhood favourite of mine. If the fruit is very ripe, mix in 30g/1oz of ground almonds or semolina to absorb the juices during cooking.

255g/9oz plain flour
30g/1oz cocoa powder
1½ tsp ground cinnamon
¼ tsp ground cloves
115g/4oz ground almonds
115g/4oz light Muscovado sugar
225g/8oz butter at room temperature, diced
1 egg, separated, plus 1 extra yolk
1 tbsp caster sugar
pouring cream, to serve

FOR THE FILLING
450g/1lb strawberries, roughly chopped
4 bananas, roughly chopped
30g/1oz caster sugar

First make the pastry: sift the flour, cocoa, spices, almonds and Muscovado sugar into a large bowl. Work in the butter and egg yolks to give a soft dough. Wrap and chill for 30 minutes.

Preheat the oven to 190C/375F/gas5.

On a lightly floured surface, roll out two-thirds of the pastry and use it to line a 25cm/10in French fluted flan tin. Add the trimmings to the reserved pastry.

Make the filling by combining the ingredients and spoon it into the pastry case.

Roll out the remaining pastry to a 25×15cm/10×6in rectangle and cut it into 10 long strips. Arrange them in a lattice effect on top of the filling. Neaten the ends and brush the pastry with lightly beaten egg white. Sprinkle with the caster sugar and bake for 40–45 minutes.

Leave to cool in the tin, then serve in wedges accompanied by pouring cream.

Strawberry and Banana Linzertorte

Mocha Whirls

You need to beat this mixture thoroughly to get it soft enough to pipe. The result is crisp, short-textured biscuits that are sandwiched together with French coffee butter cream – so much smoother than our own version.

MAKES ABOUT 14
170g/6oz unsalted butter, plus
more for greasing
55g/2oz icing sugar, sifted
150g/5½oz plain flour, sifted
15g/½oz cocoa powder, sifted
icing sugar, to dust

FOR THE COFFEE FILLING
30g/1oz caster sugar
1 egg yolk
2 tbsp hot milk
85g/3oz unsalted butter
1 tbsp strong black coffee

Preheat the oven to 180C/350F/gas4 and grease 2 baking trays with butter.

In a bowl, cream the butter and icing sugar together until very soft. Then beat in the flour and cocoa powder to give a soft piping consistency.

Using a piping bag fitted with a medium star nozzle (No. 8), pipe small 'S' shapes on the baking trays.

Bake for 15 minutes. Allow to cool slightly then transfer to a wire rack and leave to cool completely.

Make the coffee filling: whisk the sugar and egg yolk until thick and pale. Stir in the milk and transfer to a small saucepan. Cook over a gentle heat until the mixture is sufficiently thickened to coat the back of a wooden spoon.

Remove from the heat and whisk until tepid. Beat in the butter a little at a time until thick, then flavour with the coffee.

Sandwich the biscuits together with some coffee filling and leave to set. Dust with icing sugar before serving.

Mocha Whirls

Hazelnut Meringue Fingers

I'm famous amongst my friends for my meringues, yet there isn't any real secret. A pinch of salt and achieving the correct consistency is what makes them just so!

MAKES 18 PAIRS
whites of 4 eggs (175ml/6fl oz)
¼ tsp salt
225g/8oz golden caster sugar
55g/2oz roasted hazelnuts, ground
115g/4oz plain chocolate, melted
about 300ml/½pt double cream,
whipped to fairly stiff peaks

Preheat the oven to 120C/250F/gas½ and line 2 baking trays with baking parchment.

Whisk the egg whites with the salt until they form stiff peaks. Whisk in the sugar, a little at a time, until the mixture is glossy but still very stiff. Fold in the nuts.

Using a piping bag fitted with a medium star nozzle (No. 8), pipe the meringue in tight loops to make long fingers on the prepared baking trays.

Bake for about 1½ hours, until crisp and thoroughly dried out (they will lift easily from the paper). Store in an airtight container until required.

To finish: dip the ends of each meringue in melted chocolate and leave to set. Sandwich the meringues together in pairs with the whipped cream to serve.

Hazelnut Meringue Fingers

Family Favourites

*Everyone loves a steamed pudding, a
sticky fudge cake or a sugary doughnut
once in a while. Here are some
spectacular treats to satisfy the healthiest
of appetites and meet the occasional
demand for good old nursery food.*

Real Chocolate Custard with Fresh Fruit

A true egg custard is so delicious and nothing like a custard made with custard powder. It's so good it can be eaten on its own or served with a favourite fruit.

MAKES 4
4 egg yolks
55g/2oz caster sugar
450ml/¾pt milk or a combination
of milk and double cream
115g/4oz plain chocolate, broken
into pieces
1–2 bananas, peeled and sliced
8–12 strawberries, sliced
1 star fruit, sliced

Whisk the egg yolks and sugar in a bowl until pale.

Warm the milk then pour it over the egg yolks and stir well until evenly mixed. Return to the saucepan and cook over a very gentle heat, stirring constantly until lightly thickened. Do not allow to boil.

Alternatively, place the mixture in a bowl set over a saucepan of simmering water and cook, stirring, until thick enough to coat the back of a wooden spoon; or cook in a microwave oven on High, whisking every 30 seconds until thickened.

Stir in the chocolate until melted then strain the mixture through a fine sieve into a jug.

Arrange the fruit in the centre of 4 individual dishes. Pour the chocolate custard around the fruit and serve warm or cold.

Previous pages
White Chocolate Ripple Ice-cream and
Real Chocolate Custard with Fresh
Fruit

White Chocolate Ripple Ice-cream

This is an easy white chocolate ice-cream recipe made extra special by rippling it with dark chocolate sauce.

200g/7oz white chocolate, broken into pieces
200ml/7fl oz milk
3 egg yolks
200ml/7fl oz double cream

FOR THE CHOCOLATE SAUCE
85g/3oz plain chocolate
3 tbsp warmed milk
½ tbsp caster sugar
½ tbsp double cream
small knob of butter

Put the white chocolate pieces in a saucepan with the milk. Warm gently until the chocolate is just melted. Remove from the heat and stir until smooth.

Beat the egg yolks then stir in the chocolate milk to make a custard. Return the custard to the saucepan and cook, stirring all the time, over a very gentle heat, until thick enough to coat the back of a wooden spoon.

Alternatively, place the mixture in a bowl set over a saucepan of simmering water and cook, stirring, until thickened; or cook in the microwave on High for 3–4 minutes, whisking every 30 seconds until thickened.

Pass through a fine sieve and leave to go cold.

Lightly whip the double cream and fold into the chocolate mixture. Chill.

Make the sauce: warm all the ingredients together in a bain-marie until the chocolate has melted. Stir until smooth then leave to cool.

Pour the white chocolate mixture into a 900g//2lb loaf tin and then

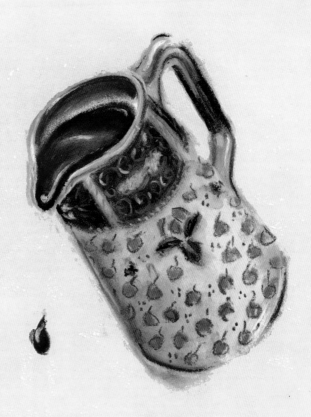

drizzle in the chocolate sauce. Using a small knife or skewer, swirl the 2 mixtures together to give a decorative ripple effect.

Freeze until hard, then serve in slices.

Alternatively, divide the white chocolate mixture between freezer-proof ramekin dishes and drizzle in the chocolate sauce in a similar way. Freeze until hard then serve in the dishes.

Sticky Chocolate Pudding à la Microwave

It's not often I'd advocate using a microwave, but this is one instance where it's better than a conventional oven. This pudding only takes 5 minutes to cook so is great for unexpected guests.

SERVES 4

115g/4oz softened butter or soft tub margarine, plus more for greasing
115g/4oz muscovado sugar
2 eggs
115g/4oz plain chocolate, broken into pieces
85g/3oz self-raising flour
30g/1oz ground almonds
4 tbsp marmalade
icing sugar, to dust
natural yogurt, crème fraîche or vanilla ice-cream, to serve

Cream the butter and sugar in a large bowl until pale and fluffy. Then beat in the eggs one at a time.

Melt the chocolate in the microwave on High for 2 minutes. Allow to cool slightly, then beat into the creamed mixture.

Fold in the flour and ground almonds then stir in the marmalade.

Transfer to a 1l/1¾pt microwave-proof dish which has been lightly greased with butter and cook on Medium for 5 minutes.

Serve warm, dusted with icing sugar and accompanied by yogurt, crème fraîche or ice-cream.

68

Apple and Apricot Pie with Chocolate Pastry

A delicious fruity pie that can be made throughout the year. It's one of my real favourites.

FOR THE FILLING
675g/1½lb cooking apples, peeled and sliced
170g/6oz dried apricots, sliced
finely grated zest of ½ a lemon
30g/1oz caster sugar
55g/2oz macaroons, crumbled
1 tbsp granulated sugar

FOR THE PASTRY
170g/6oz flour
2½ tbsp cocoa powder
pinch of salt
125g/4½oz unsalted butter
2 tbsp caster sugar
custard, cream or ice-cream to serve

In a saucepan, simmer the apples, apricots, lemon zest and caster sugar in 150ml/¼pt of water for 8–10 minutes, until thick and pulpy. Leave to go cold.

Preheat the oven to 200C/400F/gas6.

Make the pastry: sift the flour, cocoa powder and salt together. Rub in the butter, then stir in the caster sugar and 1½ tablespoons of water and mix to a firm dough.

Roll out a generous half of the pastry on a lightly floured surface and use to line a deep 20cm/8in French fluted flan tin. Trim the edges.

Sprinkle the macaroons on the base of the pastry case and spoon the filling on top.

Roll out the remaining pastry and use it to cover the top of the pie. Seal the edges well and trim off the excess pastry. Brush the surface of the pie lightly with water then sprinkle with the granulated sugar. Bake for 40 minutes.

Serve warm or cold with custard, cream or ice-cream.

Chocolate and Lime Jellies

This is a simple jelly that cleverly forms layers as it sets.

MAKES 4

170g/6oz milk chocolate, broken into pieces
2¼ tsp gelatine
2 tbsp fresh lime juice
4 tbsp whipped cream
grated chocolate or blanched julienne strips of zest from a lime, to decorate (optional)

Put the chocolate in a saucepan with 450ml/¾pt of water. Heat gently until the chocolate is melted.

In another small pan, dissolve the gelatine in the lime juice and 2 tablespoons of water over a very gentle heat. Add a little of the chocolate mixture, stir well and then return this to the bulk of the chocolate mixture.

Strain through a fine sieve and pour into four 150ml/¼pt jelly moulds or glasses. Chill until set.

Decorate with a whirl of whipped cream and some grated chocolate or lime shreds, if wished.

Really Easy Chocolate Cheesecake

As the name implies, this can be made very quickly and is always a great triumph. It doesn't have any gelatine in it so it is particularly good when entertaining vegetarian friends.

225g/8oz gingernut biscuits, crushed
115g/4oz butter, melted
170g/6oz milk chocolate
225g/8oz curd cheese
115g/4oz caster sugar
300ml/½pt Greek or thick-set natural yogurt
300ml/½pt double cream, whipped to stiff peaks

Mix the gingernut crumbs and butter together and press on the base of a 23cm/9in springform tin or loose-bottomed cake tin. Chill until firm.

Melt 115g/4oz of the chocolate and leave to cool. Coarsely grate the rest of the chocolate.

Beat together the cheese, sugar and melted chocolate, then beat in the yogurt until smooth. Fold in the whipped cream.

Spoon this mixture over the prepared base. Level the surface and chill for 4–6 hours, or preferably overnight, until set.

Sprinkle the grated chocolate evenly over the surface, then unmould and serve cut into wedges.

Bitter Chocolate Ice-cream

Home-made ice-cream is very easy to make and surpasses most commercially prepared brands. Why not have a go?

450ml/¾pt double cream
300ml/½pt milk
200g/7oz caster sugar
6 egg yolks
75g/2½oz cocoa powder, sifted

Warm the cream and milk with half the sugar in a large saucepan until the sugar is dissolved. Then bring just to the boil and remove from the heat.

Whisk the egg yolks with the remaining sugar until pale and thick. Beat in the cocoa powder until smooth.

Pour the hot cream over the chocolate mixture and stir until evenly mixed. Return the custard to the saucepan and cook, stirring all the time, over a very gentle heat until the mixture coats the back of a wooden spoon.

Alternatively, cook the custard in a bowl set over a saucepan of simmering water until thickened, or cook in the microwave on High, whisking every 30 seconds, for about 3 minutes.

Strain the custard through a fine sieve and leave to go cold. Then freeze in an ice-cream machine, or in a 1l/1¾pt rigid container, until half frozen. Take out and beat thoroughly until smooth. Return to the freezer until hard.

Serve in scoops.

Black Forest Soufflé

A classic cold soufflé is a favourite with most families. This one has the added delight of a hidden cherry filling.

225g/8oz fresh cherries, stoned
125g/4½oz caster sugar
½ tsp arrowroot
2½ tbsp Kirsch
30g/1oz cornflour
3 eggs, separated
450ml/¾pt milk
115g/4oz plain chocolate, broken
into pieces
15g/½oz powdered gelatine
150ml/¼pt double cream
grated chocolate or Chocolate
Scribbles (see page 17), to
decorate
cocoa powder, to dust

Place the cherries and 15g/½oz of the sugar in a small saucepan and heat gently until simmering.

Blend the arrowroot with a little water and stir this into the cherries until thickened. Remove from the heat and stir in 1 tablespoon of the Kirsch. Leave to go cold.

Prepare a 12.5cm/5in soufflé dish by wrapping a double thickness of baking parchment around it to extend 7.5cm/3in above the rim. Set the dish on a tray or plate.

Blend the cornflour, egg yolks and half the remaining sugar with a little cold milk until smooth.

Heat the remaining milk in a small pan, pour it into the blended cornflour and stir well. Return to the pan and cook, stirring over gentle heat until thickened.

Remove from the heat and stir in the chocolate until it melts in the heat of the custard. Beat until smooth then transfer to a large bowl, passing it through a fine sieve to make sure it is smooth. Stir in the remaining Kirsch.

Dissolve the gelatine in 3 tablespoons of water in a small saucepan over a very gentle heat. Remove from the heat and stir in a little of the chocolate mixture, then stir this back into the bulk of the mixture. Chill until starting to set.

Whisk the egg whites until stiff then whisk in the remaining sugar, a little at a time, until thick and glossy. Fold the egg whites into the chocolate mixture until evenly combined.

Spoon the cherries into the soufflé dish then top with the chocolate mixture and leave in the refrigerator for 4–6 hours, preferably overnight, until set.

Alternatively, set a thin jam jar or glass in the centre of the soufflé dish and pop in a few ice cubes to secure it. Pour the chocolate mixture around the jar and leave it to set firm. Remove the jar by pouring a little hot water into it and then twisting it out of the soufflé. Fill the recess left by the jar with the cherries.

Carefully peel away the baking parchment. Lightly whip the cream and spread a thin layer over the top of the soufflé. Using a fine knife, mark a lattice effect on top.

Fill a piping bag fitted with a star nozzle with the remaining whipped cream and pipe rosettes around the edge of the soufflé. Decorate with grated chocolate or Chocolate Scribbles and dust with cocoa powder. Chill again until ready to serve.

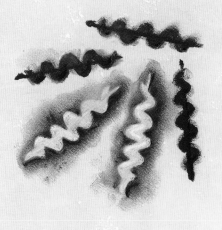

Previous pages
Chocolate Multi-Decker Fudge Cake
and Black Forest Soufflé

Chocolate Multi-Decker Fudge Cake

I'm always trying new recipes for chocolate cake and frequently discarding them, and I'm not the only one. I remember complimenting a chef on his chocolate cake only to be told that he'd been on a similar search and decided he couldn't better a superior American packet mix to which he added ground almonds! I'm pleased to say I'm happy with this one!

170g/6oz butter, softened, plus
more for greasing
170g/6oz plain chocolate, broken
into pieces
150ml/¼pt boiling water
350g/12oz plain flour
55g/2oz cocoa powder
2 tsp baking powder
4 tsp bicarbonate of soda
350g/12oz light Muscovado sugar
3 eggs, beaten
150ml/¼pt milk
whipped cream or ice-cream, to
serve

FOR THE FILLING
225g/8oz plain chocolate, broken
into pieces
15g/½oz butter
175ml/6fl oz soured cream
30g/1oz icing sugar, sifted
¼ tsp salt

FOR THE ICING
255g/9oz caster sugar
150ml/¼pt water
200g/7oz plain chocolate, broken
into pieces

Preheat the oven to 180C/350F/gas4. Grease two 22cm/8½in round cake tins or springform tins with butter and line their bases with baking parchment.

Place the chocolate in a bowl and pour over the boiling water. Leave to melt and then stir until smooth.

Sift the flour, cocoa powder, baking powder and bicarbonate of soda together into a bowl.

In another bowl, cream the butter with half the sugar until pale and fluffy. Beat in the rest of the sugar until the mixture is pale. (It can be creamed all in one go, but it does take a very long time.)

Beat the eggs into the creamed mixture a little at a time. Then fold in alternating small amounts of the flour mixture, the chocolate mixture and the milk until all are evenly combined.

Divide the mixture between the prepared tins, level the surface and make a slight depression in the centre of each one. Bake for 45–50 minutes, until well risen and just firm to the touch.

Allow to cool slightly in the tins, then unmould on wire racks and leave to cool completely. Invert the tins over the top of the cakes while they are cooling to help keep them moist.

Make the filling: melt the chocolate and butter together in a bowl set over simmering water. Then beat in the soured cream, icing sugar and salt until smooth. Leave to cool.

Split each cake in half horizontally and sandwich them all together with 3 layers of the filling. Set the cake on a cooling tray over a plastic tray.

Make the icing: place all the ingredients in a saucepan and heat gently until the sugar dissolves. Stir thoroughly, then bring to the boil and boil for a few minutes until the temperature on a sugar thermometer reaches 116C/240F (soft ball stage).

Leave to cool slightly until syrupy, then pour the icing over the cake so that it covers the sides. Try not to use a knife on the top to spread it, but it will be necessary on the sides. If necessary, collect excess icing in the tray and warm it again. Repeat the coating process. Leave to set.

Serve cut in wedges, accompanied by whipped cream or ice-cream.

Note: make double the quantity of filling and use to fill and cover the cake instead of using the chocolate icing if you prefer.

Doughnut Surprises

Light, sugary doughnuts with a surprise chocolate custard centre – so bite into them carefully!

MAKES 8

15g/½oz fresh yeast or 8g/¼oz dried yeast or 1 sachet of easy-blend yeast
4 tbsp lukewarm milk or water
225g/8oz strong plain flour
½ tsp salt
55g/2oz caster sugar
1 egg, beaten
2 tbsp vegetable oil
finely grated zest of ½ a lemon
vegetable oil, for deep-frying
caster or icing sugar, to dust

FOR THE CHOCOLATE CUSTARD
150ml/¼pt milk
55g/2oz milk chocolate, broken into pieces
1 tbsp custard powder

Mix the fresh or dried yeast with the milk or water. Sift the flour, salt and sugar into a bowl, make a well in the centre and pour in the yeast mixture. Leave in a warm place for about 20 minutes, until frothy. If using easy-blend yeast, mix it with the dry ingredients and omit the frothing.

Add the beaten egg, oil and lemon zest and mix to a soft dough. Beat well until smooth. Then cover and leave to rise in a warm place for ¾–1 hour, or until doubled in size.

Make the custard: in a saucepan, warm two-thirds of the milk with the chocolate until melted. Mix the remaining milk and custard powder in a large bowl until smooth then pour in the chocolate milk. Stir well then return to the saucepan and cook over gentle heat, stirring all the time, until thickened. Cover and leave to go cold.

On a lightly floured surface, knead the dough and then divide it into 8 pieces. Roll out each one to a round and place a spoonful of custard in the centre. Draw up the edges to completely encase the custard and seal well.

Place the doughnuts on an oiled baking tray, cover and leave in a warm place for 15–30 minutes, until well risen (the dough should spring back when pressed with a fingertip).

Heat the oil to 180C/360F (or until a small cube of dry bread browns in 60 seconds) and fry the doughnuts for about 5 minutes until golden brown.

Drain on paper towels, then roll in caster sugar or dust with icing sugar. Serve fresh.

Doughnut Surprises and Chocolate and Peanut Crackles

Chocolate and Peanut Crackles

Kids' stuff but ever popular, these crackles have the added goodness of peanuts and peanut butter.

MAKES 15
140g/5oz golden syrup
85g/3oz golden caster sugar
115g/4oz unsweetened crunchy peanut butter
115g/4oz plain chocolate, melted
85g/3oz cornflakes
55g/2oz roasted peanuts

Warm the golden syrup and sugar together in a saucepan then stir in the peanut butter and mix thoroughly. Remove from the heat and stir in the chocolate, cornflakes and peanuts until evenly combined.

Divide the mixture between 15 paper cases. Leave to go cold and firm. Store in an airtight container.

Neapolitan Steamed Pudding

Steamed puddings make wonderful family fare and this one is no exception packed with fruit and chocolate drops.

SERVES 4–6
85g/3oz softened butter or soft tub margarine, plus more for greasing
115g/4oz clear honey
2 eggs
170g/6oz wholemeal flour
1 tsp baking powder
55g/2oz glacé cherries, quartered
55g/2oz cut mixed peel
55g/2oz chocolate drops
55g/2oz shelled walnuts, chopped
1 tbsp milk
vanilla or chocolate custard, to serve

Lightly grease a 900ml/1½pt pudding basin with some butter or margarine.

Cream the butter or margarine in a bowl until light, then beat in the honey followed by the eggs. Fold in the flour and baking powder. Stir in the cherries, peel, chocolate drops and walnuts and mix to a soft dropping consistency with the milk.

Transfer the mixture to the prepared basin and level the surface.

Cut a large round of kitchen foil or greaseproof paper and lightly grease it with butter or margarine. Fold a pleat in the centre to allow for expansion during cooking and cover the basin tightly. Secure with a rubber band or string.

Place the basin in a steamer or large saucepan and pour boiling water around it to come at least two-thirds of the way up the basin.

Cover and cook for about 1½ hours, adding extra water to the pan as necessary, until risen and just firm to the touch.

Leave to cool slightly, then unmould on a serving plate. Serve with vanilla or chocolate custard.

Neapolitan Steamed Pudding

Chocolate and Apple Pancakes

A recent visit to Normandy gave me the idea for these pancakes – chocolate seems to combine well with lots of fruits, in this case, apple purée.

SERVES 8

FOR THE BATTER
115g/4oz plain flour
pinch of salt
1 egg plus 1 extra yolk
1 tbsp vegetable oil
300ml/½pt milk
55g/2oz unsalted butter
1 tbsp granulated sugar
fresh cream, crème fraîche or ice-cream, to serve

FOR THE FILLING
450g/1lb cooking apples, peeled, cored and chopped
30–55g/1–2oz sugar
170g/6oz chocolate spread

Put the flour, salt, egg and the extra yolk, the oil and milk in a blender or food processor and blend until smooth.

Alternatively, sift the flour and salt into a bowl. Make a well in the centre, add the eggs and some of the milk. Whisk to give a thick smooth batter, adding the rest of the milk a little at a time. Set aside.

Make the filling: in a small pan, cook the apples with the sugar and 4 tablespoons of water for about 3 minutes until soft. Leave to cool.

Heat a tiny amount of butter in an 18cm/7in pancake pan and pour in a small amount of batter, swirling it round to cover the bottom of the pan.

Cook until golden on one side, then flip it over and cook the other side until lightly golden. Repeat with the remaining batter to make 16 small pancakes in all.

Preheat the oven to 220C/425F/gas7 and grease an ovenproof dish with a little of the remaining butter.

Place a spoonful of the cooked apples and a little chocolate spread in the centre of each pancake, then fold in the sides to encase the filling.

Set the pancakes in the prepared dish. Melt the remaining butter and brush the pancakes with it. Sprinkle with the granulated sugar.

Cook the pancakes in the oven for 15 minutes, until warmed through. Serve with fresh cream, crème fraîche or ice-cream.

Steamed Chocolate Puddings with Caramel Sauce

Steamed puddings are always popular; these are especially light because they don't have any flour in them but rely on the lightness of breadcrumbs and whisked egg whites. Creamy caramel sauce gives a good contrast, but you could also use the chocolate sauce on page 19.

MAKES 8
*85g/3oz butter, softened, plus
more for greasing
85g/3oz plain chocolate, broken
into pieces
150ml/¼pt milk
140g/5oz fresh white breadcrumbs
or stale cake crumbs or a mixture
of the two
85g/3oz caster sugar
2 eggs, separated*

FOR THE CARAMEL SAUCE
*170g/6oz caster sugar
115g/4oz unsalted butter, diced
300ml/½pt double cream*

Grease 8 dariole moulds with butter and cut 8 pieces of foil or grease-proof paper just big enough to cover their tops and come down the sides a little. Grease each of these lightly with butter.

Place the chocolate and milk in a small saucepan and heat gently, stirring until the chocolate has melted. Bring just to the boil then remove from the heat and add the breadcrumbs. Leave to go cold.

Prepare a steamer or a wide shallow pan with boiling water.

Cream the butter and sugar until pale and fluffy then beat in the egg yolks and the chocolate mixture. Whisk the egg whites until stiff and then fold them into the chocolate mixture.

Divide this between the prepared moulds, cover with foil or grease-proof paper, buttered side down, and secure as necessary with rubber bands or string. Steam for about 20 minutes until risen and just firm to the touch.

Meanwhile in a small saucepan, make the sauce: dissolve the sugar in 6 tablespoons of water over a gentle heat. Then bring to the boil and cook until it turns a rich caramel colour.

Remove from the heat and stir in the butter until melted. Then stir in half the cream to give a smooth sauce. Warm gently, stirring occasionally.

Unmould the puddings on individual plates and serve drizzled with caramel sauce and the remaining cream.

Apricot and Raspberry Crumble

The combination of apricot and raspberry is a particularly good one, but the apricots may be replaced by an equal quantity of peach, nectarine or plum. Out of season use half the amount of dried apricots and soak them overnight in boiling water.

SERVES 6–8

450g/1lb fresh apricots, quartered and stoned
225g/8oz fresh or frozen raspberries
85g/3oz sugar
1 tbsp lemon juice
140g/5oz plain flour
30g/1oz cocoa powder
115g/4oz Demerara sugar
55g/2oz butter at room temperature, diced
55g/2oz pine kernels
custard, cream or ice-cream, to serve

Preheat the oven to 190C/375F/gas5.

Combine the fruit, sugar and lemon juice and place in an ovenproof serving dish with a capacity of about 1l/1¾pt.

Sift the flour and cocoa powder into a bowl. Stir in the sugar and rub in the butter until the mixture resembles fine crumbs. Stir in the pine kernels.

Sprinkle the crumble mixture on top of the fruit and press down lightly. Bake for about 40 minutes, until the crumble topping is quite firm and crunchy.

Serve with custard, cream or ice-cream.

Apricot and Raspberry Crumble

Chocolate Rippled Bread and Butter Pudding

Bread and butter pudding seems to have reached great culinary heights over the last few years. It has always been a favourite of mine – this time it's made with chocolate sandwiches!

SERVES 6–8
6 slices of white bread, crusts removed
45g/1½oz butter, softened
85g/3oz plain chocolate, grated
300ml/½pt single or double cream
300ml/½pt milk
6 egg yolks
30g/1oz caster sugar, plus 1 tbsp for sprinkling
55g/2oz mixed dried fruit
freshly grated nutmeg
pouring cream, to serve (optional)

Spread the bread with butter then make 3 sandwiches using the chocolate as filling. Alternatively, cream the butter and beat in the chocolate then use this as the filling. Cut each sandwich in quarters to make 12 triangles in all.

Arrange the bread attractively in a 1l/1¾pt ovenproof dish.

In a saucepan, bring the cream and milk just to the boil. Whisk the egg yolks and 30g/1oz sugar together in a bowl. Stir in the warm cream and milk. Strain the mixture over the bread and sprinkle with the dried fruit and a little nutmeg. Leave to stand for 15 minutes.

Preheat the oven to 220C/425F/gas7.

Cover the pudding with foil and place in a large roasting tin. Pour boiling water into the tin to come at least half-way up the dish.

Bake for 30 minutes then remove the foil, sprinkle with the remaining 1 tablespoon of sugar and bake for a further 15 minutes, until crisp and golden on the top and lightly set.

Serve warm with pouring cream if you want to be totally indulgent!

Chocolate Rippled Bread and Butter Pudding

Pear and Chocolate Upside-down Pudding

A light chocolate sponge baked on top of lightly caramelized pear slices – perfect for a winter's day.

SERVES 4–6

55g/2oz butter, plus more for greasing
4 ripe conference pears
115g/4oz golden caster sugar
2 eggs
45g/1½oz plain flour
15g/½oz cocoa powder
vanilla custard, cream or ice-cream, to serve

Preheat the oven to 200C/400F/gas6. Grease a 20–22cm/8–8½in loose-bottomed cake tin with butter and line the base with baking parchment.

Peel, core and slice the pears and arrange them attractively in the bottom of the tin.

In a small pan, melt the butter with half the sugar. Stir until well mixed and pour over the pears.

Whisk the eggs with the remaining sugar in a bowl set over simmering water, until thick and foamy (the whisk should leave a trail in the mixture).

Remove from the heat and sift in the flour and cocoa powder. Fold in well. Pour the mixture over the fruit and level the surface.

Bake for about 30 minutes until risen and just firm to the touch. Leave to cool in the tin for 5 minutes.

Unmould by inverting on a serving plate and serve with vanilla custard, cream or ice-cream.

Pear and Chocolate Upside-down Pudding

Dinner Party Desserts

For the true chocoholic, dinner parties provide the perfect opportunity for unmitigated indulgence. These frail-looking concoctions, as rich as they are sleek, will break every vow of dinner-time temperance, and seal your day with a luscious kiss.

Wicked Chocolate Fondue

This must be one of the easiest desserts in the world and it relies totally on the quality of the chocolate. Find one you really like from the overwhelming choice and indulge yourself.

225g/8oz plain chocolate (the darker, the better), broken into pieces
250ml/8fl oz double or single cream
fresh fruits, such as strawberries, quartered red plums, halved figs or seedless grapes, to serve

Place the chocolate pieces in a saucepan with the cream. Warm gently until the chocolate has melted, then beat thoroughly until glossy.

Serve at once with a selection of prepared fruits. Spike a piece of fruit on a fork, dip it in the fondue and eat immediately.

Previous pages
Wicked Chocolate Fondue, Chocolate Purses and Pecan Mud Pie

Pecan Mud Pie

Pecan pie is a particular favourite of mine – and this one flavoured with chocolate is quite something!

FOR THE PASTRY
170g/6oz plain flour
pinch of salt
115g/4oz unsalted butter
30g/1oz caster sugar

FOR THE FILLING
225g/8oz butter, diced
170g/6oz plain chocolate, broken into pieces
125ml/4fl oz light corn syrup, maple syrup or golden syrup
4 eggs, beaten
115g/4oz pecan halves

First make the pastry: sift the flour and salt into a bowl and rub in the butter. Stir in the sugar and add 1 tablespoon of water. Mix to a firm dough.

On a lightly floured surface, roll out the pastry and use to line a 24cm/9½in fluted flan dish. Trim and neaten the edges. Prick the base with a fork and chill until required.

Preheat the oven to 190C/375F/gas5.

Make the filling: melt the butter and chocolate with the syrup over a gentle heat. Leave to cool. Stir in the beaten eggs and pour the filling into the prepared pastry case.

Arrange the pecan halves on the surface, then bake for about 30 minutes until lightly set. Leave to cool.

Paradise Ice-cream Gâteau

The combination of coconut and chocolate is delightful in this rich ice-cream gâteau. Make it at least 24 hours before required, or it will keep in the freezer for up to 1 month if properly wrapped.

*1 quantity Bitter Chocolate
Ice-cream (see page 71)*

FOR THE COCONUT ICE-CREAM
*300ml/½pt milk
450ml/¾pt double cream
85g/3oz desiccated coconut (or
peeled and freshly grated coconut,
if possible)
170g/6oz caster sugar
6 egg yolks*

FOR THE TRUFFLES
*140g/5oz plain chocolate
5 tbsp whipping or double cream*

FOR THE BISCUIT BASE
*115g/4oz digestive biscuits,
crushed
115g/4oz gingernuts, crushed
30g/1oz light Muscovado sugar
85g/3oz butter, melted*

TO SERVE
*whipped cream
toasted coconut flakes (optional)*

First make the coconut ice-cream: place the milk, two-thirds of the cream, the coconut and half the sugar in a saucepan and bring just to the boil.

Whisk the egg yolks and remaining sugar until thick and pale. Then pour the hot cream in and stir until evenly mixed.

Return to the saucepan and cook, stirring all the time, over a very gentle heat, until thick enough to coat the back of a wooden spoon.

Alternatively, cook the mixture in a bain-marie or in the microwave on High, whisking every 30 seconds, for 3–4 minutes.

Leave to cool then chill until completely cold. Whip the remaining cream lightly and fold this into the mixture.

Freeze in an ice-cream machine, or in a rigid container, until half frozen. Beat thoroughly, then return to the freezer until quite firm.

Make the truffles: melt the chocolate in the cream over a gentle heat, then beat until smooth. Chill for about 30 minutes, until set. Shape into 20 small balls and chill again until required.

Line a 23cm/9in loose-bottomed cake tin with baking parchment. Spoon in a generous half of the coconut ice-cream then dot the chocolate truffles over the mixture. Top with the remaining ice-cream and level the surface. Freeze until firm.

Soften the chocolate ice-cream, then beat until smooth. Spread it on top of the coconut ice-cream. Level the surface. Return to the freezer.

Make the base: combine all the ingredients and sprinkle them on top of the chocolate ice-cream. Press down firmly and level the surface. Freeze for at least 4 hours, preferably overnight, until hard.

Unmould on a serving plate and decorate with whirls of cream and toasted coconut flakes, if using.

Chocolate Crème Caramels

Crème caramel, if properly made, still remains an all-time favourite of mine. The addition of chocolate is a basic variation to a delicious dessert.

MAKES 7
125g/4½oz caster sugar
575ml/1pt milk or single cream or
a mixture of the two
½ vanilla pod, split, or a large
strip of zest from an orange
55g/2oz plain chocolate, grated
4 eggs

Preheat the oven to 160C/325F/gas3.

Place 115g/4oz of the sugar in a small saucepan and heat gently without stirring until the sugar is dissolved and cooked to a medium caramel colour.

Pour the caramel into seven 125ml/4fl oz individual ramekin dishes and swirl each one so that the caramel covers the base.

In a saucepan, warm the milk with the vanilla pod or orange rind until it just comes to the boil. Remove from the heat, stir in the chocolate and leave to infuse for 10 minutes.

Whisk the eggs with the remaining sugar. Pour on the milk and stir thoroughly. Strain the mixture into the ramekin dishes and place in a large roasting tin.

Pour boiling water into the roasting tin to come at least half-way up the sides of the ramekins. Bake for about 20 minutes until just set. Test with a small sharp knife inserted into the centre of the custard; if it comes out clean the custard is ready.

Chill until required. Unmould on individual plates to serve.

Chocolate Purses

Egg-white pancakes are an Asian innovation that I use very successfully to make these sweet chocolate purses. They can be prepared in advance, but must be fried just before serving so that they are crisp and warm.

SERVES 4
175ml/6fl oz egg whites (from 4–5
size-2 eggs)
1 tsp cornflour
1 tsp cocoa powder, sifted
30g/1oz unsalted butter
8 whole almonds, toasted
4 ripe plums or apricots, halved
and stoned
2 vanilla pods
sunflower oil, for deep-frying
icing sugar, for dusting

FOR THE CUSTARD SAUCE
300ml/½pt milk
2 tbsp caster sugar
1 tsp cornflour
2 egg yolks

Mix the egg whites, cornflour and cocoa powder together thoroughly with 3 tablespoons of cold water.

Heat a tiny amount of butter in a 15cm/6in non-stick frying pan and add about one-eighth of the mixture, swirling it over the base of the pan to make a thin pancake. Cook on the one side only until set, then remove from the pan. Use the remaining mixture to make 7 more pancakes.

Place a whole almond on each plum or apricot half and set it in the middle of each pancake.

Cut each vanilla pod in half lengthwise and scrape out the vanilla seeds. Reserve these for the custard. Cut each piece of pod in half lengthwise to give 8 lengths in all.

Draw up the sides of the pancakes around the fruit and, using a piece of vanilla pod, tie each one up like a purse.

Make the custard: heat the milk with the reserved vanilla seeds. Beat together the sugar, cornflour and egg yolks then pour on the hot milk and mix well. Return to the saucepan and cook, stirring all the time, until thickened. Keep warm.

Heat the oil to 190C/375F (or until a cube of dry bread browns in 40 seconds) and deep-fry the purses until crisp. Drain on paper towels and dust generously with icing sugar.

Chocolate Purses

Set 2 purses on each warmed plate and spoon a little sauce around each one to serve.

White Chocolate Roulade

It took me quite a while to perfect this white roulade with its subtle sweet flavour. It makes a welcome change from the dark chocolate variety.

SERVES 6–8
170g/6oz finest quality white chocolate
5 eggs, separated
170g/6oz golden caster sugar
1 tbsp cornflour, sifted
1 tbsp flour, sifted
30g/1oz ground almonds
150ml/¼pt double cream, whipped
150ml/¼pt Greek yogurt
butter, for greasing
icing sugar, to decorate
fresh redcurrants, to serve
(optional)

Preheat the oven to 180C/350F/gas4. Grease a 38×23cm/15×9in Swiss roll tin with butter and line it with baking parchment.

Gently warm the chocolate with 3 tablespoons of water and stir together until melted and smooth.

Whisk the egg whites until stiff, then whisk in about one-quarter of the sugar, a little at a time, until thick and glossy.

Using the same whisk, whisk the egg yolks and remaining sugar together until thick and pale. Stir in the chocolate mixture until evenly combined. Fold in the cornflour and flour, followed by the whisked egg whites.

Transfer the mixture to the prepared tin and level the surface. Bake for 15–20 minutes, until just firm to the touch. Cover with a sheet of baking parchment and a damp tea-towel and leave to cool completely.

Sprinkle a sheet of baking parchment with the ground almonds and unmould the sponge on it. Mix the whipped cream and yogurt together and spread this over the sponge. Trim the edges. Roll up, starting at a short end.

Dust liberally with icing sugar and serve with redcurrants, if using.

Note: for a dark chocolate roulade, replace the white chocolate with plain chocolate and omit the cornflour and flour. Unmould on a sheet of paper dusted with icing sugar instead of ground almonds.

White Chocolate Mousses with Bramble Sauce and White Chocolate Roulade

White Chocolate Mousses with Bramble Sauce

White chocolate is very sweet, so this sharp fruity sauce is a perfect partner.

MAKES 6

170g/6oz finest quality white chocolate, broken into pieces
225g/8oz fromage frais
55g/2oz curd cheese
whites of 2 eggs
125ml/4fl oz double cream
18 brambles, to decorate
6 small sprigs of mint, to decorate

FOR THE BRAMBLE SAUCE
350g/12oz brambles
2–3 tbsp icing sugar, sifted

Melt the chocolate in a bowl set over a saucepan of simmering water or in the microwave. Allow to cool slightly, then beat in the fromage frais and curd cheese.

Whisk the egg whites to stiff peaks and lightly whip the cream. Fold the cream in to the chocolate mixture, followed by the egg whites. Spoon into 6 individual glasses or small dishes and chill for at least 1 hour, or until required.

Make the sauce: purée the brambles with icing sugar to taste, then pass the sauce through a fine sieve to remove the seeds.

To serve, decorate each mousse with three brambles and a sprig of mint. Serve the sauce separately.

Gâteau Lany

Lany is a great friend of mine and this is her favourite chocolate dessert, which is much admired by all her guests – including me! She likes it best when it's been left in the fridge for 24 hours to soften the layers; I like mine crisper – you can decide for yourself!

FOR THE SAUCE
225g/8oz plain chocolate, broken into pieces
115g/4oz caster sugar
1 tbsp cocoa powder, sifted

FOR THE PASTRY
255g/9oz plain flour
30g/1oz cornflour
pinch of salt
140g/5oz butter at room temperature, diced

FOR THE FILLING
300ml/½pt double cream
2 tbsp Crème d'Abricot, brandy or Cointreau

TO DECORATE
Chocolate Curls or Shavings made from 115g/4oz plain chocolate (see pages 16 and 19)

First make the sauce: mix all the ingredients in a saucepan with 150ml/¼pt water and heat gently, stirring to give a smooth sauce. Divide in half in separate bowls and leave to cool to room temperature.

Preheat the oven to 220C/425F/gas7.

Make the pastry: sift together the dry ingredients and rub in the butter until the mixture resembles fine crumbs. Stir in one of the bowls of chocolate sauce and mix well until thoroughly combined.

Cut out three 30×17.5cm/12×7in rectangles of baking parchment and place on separate baking trays.

Divide the chocolate pastry into 3 equal portions and press one evenly on each piece of paper to cover it completely. Bake for 10 minutes. Then, while still warm, trim the edges of each and cut them in half lengthwise. Leave to cool.

Whip the cream until stiff, then fold in the remaining chocolate sauce and liqueur. Use a generous half of this to sandwich the 6 layers of pastry together. Cover the top and sides with the remaining filling.

Decorate the top of the gâteau with the Chocolate Curls and chill for 4–6 hours. Serve cut into slices.

Mint Surprise Mousses

There's no doubt that these are a little tricky to make as the 'surprise' chocolate sauce has to be carefully piped into the centre of the delicate mint mousse – but please don't let that stop you trying them – the reward is in the result! Leaf gelatine is not so easy to buy but is much easier to use than powder gelatine and has a more delicate texture.

MAKES 6

FOR THE CHOCOLATE SAUCE
30g/1oz cocoa powder, sifted
55g/2oz caster sugar
15g/½oz plain chocolate

FOR THE MOUSSE
125ml/4fl oz milk
55g/2oz white chocolate, broken into pieces
2 gelatine leaves or ¾ tsp powdered gelatine
2 eggs, separated
3 tbsp Crème de Menthe
½ tsp lemon juice
125ml/4fl oz double cream, lightly whipped
vegetable oil, for greasing
whipped cream, to decorate
6 mint sprigs, to decorate

First make the chocolate sauce: mix the cocoa to a paste with 3 tablespoons of water. Dissolve the sugar in another 3 tablespoons of water in a small saucepan over a gentle heat. Stir in the cocoa paste and bring to the boil, stirring constantly.

Remove the sauce from the heat and stir in the chocolate until melted. Pass through a fine sieve and leave to go cold.

Make the mousses: warm the milk and white chocolate together in a small pan until the chocolate melts.

Soften the gelatine powder in 2 tablespoons of water. If, however, you are using gelatine leaves, put them in enough water to cover them.

In a bowl, whisk the egg yolks together with the milk mixture.

Return this to the saucepan and cook over a gentle heat, stirring all the time, until lightly thickened. Do not let the mixture boil. Remove from the heat.

If using the gelatine leaves, drain them and stir them into the egg mixture until dissolved; if using powdered gelatine, warm it gently until dissolved then stir it into the egg mixture. Strain the mixture through a fine sieve, then flavour it with the Crème de Menthe and lemon juice, and chill.

When the mixture is beginning to set, fold in the whipped cream. Whisk the egg whites until stiff then fold them into the mixture. Divide the mixture between six 150ml/¼pt lightly oiled moulds.

Make a greaseproof paper piping bag but do not snip the end off. Fill the bag with the cool chocolate sauce. Just before using, snip off the end but keep a teaspoon over it so that the sauce does not drop out.

Push the tip of the piping bag into the centre of one mousse below the surface and squeeze out about one-sixth of the sauce. Carefully lift the bag away and have the teaspoon ready to cover the tip. Repeat with the remaining mousses.

Cover and chill for at least 4 hours, preferably overnight, until completely set.

Unmould on individual serving plates. Top with a rosette of whipped cream and a mint sprig.

Lemon Tartlets

The tangy flavour and wonderfully delicate consistency of this lemon filling marries perfectly with the dark chocolate pastry. The cases may be prepared up to 24 hours in advance, but please cook the filling just before required to give a perfect result.

MAKES 6

FOR THE PASTRY
150g/5½oz plain flour
25g/¾oz cocoa powder
45g/1½oz caster sugar
100g/3½oz butter at room temperature, diced
2 tbsp beaten egg

FOR THE FILLING
finely grated zest and juice of 2 large lemons
150ml/¼pt double cream
170g/6oz caster sugar
4 eggs

TO DECORATE
icing sugar
6 small non-poisonous leaves such as lemon
about 6 tbsp whipped cream
6 Chocolate Butterflies (see page 17)

First make the pastry: sift the flour and cocoa powder together into a bowl and stir in the sugar. Rub in the butter until the mixture resembles fine crumbs. Add the egg and work together to form a firm dough. Wrap and chill for 20 minutes.

On a lightly floured surface, roll out the pastry and use it to line 6 deep 10cm/4in individual tartlet tins. Prick the bases with a fork then chill for at least 20 minutes.

Preheat the oven to 190C/375F/gas5.

Line the pastry cases with foil or greaseproof paper, weight with beans and bake them blind for 20 minutes, removing the baking beans and paper after 10 minutes. Reduce the oven temperature to 160C/325F/gas3.

Make the filling by whisking together the ingredients. Pour it into the pastry cases and then bake them for 15–20 minutes in the cooler oven until just set. Leave to cool in the tins.

Unmould on individual plates. Decorate with a rosette of whipped cream, a small leaf and a Chocolate Butterfly.

Lemon Tartlets

Chocolate Terrine

It's always useful to have a dessert on standby in the freezer – and this one is just perfect. It appeals to all ages and can be decorated to suit the occasion.

SERVES 8
170g/6oz plain chocolate, broken into pieces
85g/3oz unsalted butter
3 eggs, separated
45g/1½oz icing sugar, sifted
2 tbsp cocoa powder, sifted
200ml/7fl oz double cream, plus extra to decorate
fresh fruit, such as orange segments, to decorate
chocolate decorations (see page 16)

In a small pan, melt the chocolate with half the butter over a gentle heat.

In a bowl, beat the egg yolks with the icing sugar until thick and pale. In another bowl, beat the remaining butter with the cocoa powder until it has a soft dropping consistency. Pour this into the egg yolk mixture together with the contents of the pan. Mix until smooth.

Whisk the egg whites until stiff and lightly whip the cream. Fold the cream into the chocolate mixture, followed by the egg whites.

Line a 900g/2lb loaf tin with clingfilm. Pour the mixture into it and smooth the top. Cover and freeze for at least 4–6 hours, or preferably overnight, until hard.

Unmould and allow to soften slightly then cut in thin slices. Serve the slices on individual plates, decorated with whipped cream, fresh fruit of your choice and chocolate decorations such as leaves or scribbles.

Prune and Chocolate Tart

This tart is not only for chocolate lovers but also 'nut freaks', just like me, as the pastry is made with ground almonds and the prunes are stuffed with chocolate almond paste! Like all pastries this tart is best served fresh.

SERVES 8–10
32 ready-to-eat pitted prunes
200ml/7fl oz red wine
170g/6oz plain or milk chocolate
115g/4oz ground almonds
30g/1oz caster sugar
white of 1 egg
6 tbsp redcurrant jelly
2 tbsp lemon juice or water

FOR THE PASTRY
170g/6oz plain flour
115g/4oz butter at room temperature, diced
45g/1½oz ground almonds
45g/1½oz caster sugar
1 egg yolk

FOR THE CUSTARD
4 tsp custard powder
150ml/¼pt milk
150ml/¼pt double cream
1 tsp caster sugar

Soak the prunes in the wine in a saucepan for 2–3 hours.

Cover, bring to the boil and simmer for 5 minutes. Leave to cool then drain, reserving the liquid.

Make the pastry: sift the flour into a bowl. Rub in the butter until the mixture resembles fine crumbs then stir in the ground almonds and sugar. Add the egg yolk and work the mixture to a firm dough. Wrap and chill for 30 minutes.

On a lightly floured surface, roll out the pastry and use to line a 25cm/ 10in French fluted flan tin. Prick the base with a fork then chill for 30 minutes.

Make the custard: blend the custard powder with a little of the milk in a bowl until smooth. Heat the remaining milk in a small saucepan and then pour this into the custard mixture. Stir well and return to the saucepan. Cook, stirring constantly, until thickened. Cover and leave to cool.

Whip the cream with the sugar until stiff. Beat the custard until smooth, then fold in the cream. Leave in a cool place.

Preheat the oven to 190C/375F/gas5.

Line the pastry case with foil or greaseproof paper and weight with beans. Bake blind for 25–30 minutes, removing the baking beans and paper after 15 minutes, until golden. Leave to cool. Then melt one-third of the chocolate and brush the base of the pastry case with it. Leave in a cool place until the chocolate is set.

Make a chocolate almond paste by grating the remaining chocolate and mixing it with the ground almonds, sugar and egg white to make a paste. Divide into 32 pieces and use to stuff the prunes.

Spread the cooled custard over the base of the flan then arrange the prunes decoratively on top.

Warm the reserved prune liquid with the redcurrant jelly and lemon juice, stirring, until smooth. Bring to the boil and continue to bubble until slightly syrupy. Allow to cool slightly and use to glaze the top of the flan.

Serve as soon as the glaze is set.

Rich Chocolate Pots

If you have any sturdy coffee cups that can withstand the heat of the oven, then use them to cook the custard in – it's an amusing way to serve these delicate little desserts.

SERVES 4
300ml/½pt single cream
115g/4oz plain chocolate, broken into pieces
4 egg yolks
1 tbsp strong black coffee
fresh berries, to serve (optional)
plain sweet biscuits, to serve

Preheat the oven to 160C/325F/gas3.

In a small pan, warm the cream and chocolate together until the chocolate just melts. Stir until smooth.

Whisk the egg yolks and stir in the chocolate milk followed by the coffee. Strain the mixture through a fine sieve and then pour it into 4 custard cups or small ramekin dishes.

Stand them in a roasting tin and pour in hot water to come at least two-thirds of the way up the sides of the dishes.

Bake for about 25 minutes, until lightly set. Leave to cool.

Serve lightly chilled and topped with fresh berries, if using, accompanied by plain sweet biscuits.

Chocolate Concord

Chocolate Concord

This wonderful creation combines chocolate meringue with a wicked chocolate mousse to give a delightful dessert. Serve it in slices with pouring cream to make it perfect! It's also a great way to use up egg whites, so keep any you have and store them in the fridge for a few days or in the freezer until required. Thaw them at room temperature.

FOR THE MERINGUE
45g/1½oz cocoa powder
140g/5oz icing sugar
200ml/7fl oz egg whites (about 5 size-2 eggs)
140g/5oz granulated sugar

FOR THE MOUSSE
170g/6oz plain chocolate, broken into pieces
100g/3½oz butter
3 eggs, separated, plus the white of 1 extra egg
30g/1oz caster sugar
icing sugar, to dust
cocoa powder, to dust

Preheat the oven to 150C/300F/gas2. Cut three 30×12.5cm/12×5in rectangles from baking parchment and place on 3 separate baking trays.

Make the meringue: sift the cocoa powder and icing sugar together. Whisk the egg whites for about 5 minutes until stiff, adding 2 tablespoons of the granulated sugar halfway through. Whisk in the remaining sugar a little at a time, then fold in the cocoa sugar until evenly combined.

Using a piping bag fitted with a 1cm/½in plain nozzle, cover each piece of baking parchment with meringue working in a continuous close backwards and forwards movement.

Bake for 1¼ hours then leave to cool. Trim each meringue to a 25×10cm/10×4in rectangle. Reserve all the meringue trimmings and crush coarsely.

Make the mousse: melt the chocolate and stir in the butter. Leave the mixture to cool, then beat in the egg yolks.

Whisk the egg whites until stiff, then whisk in the sugar a little at a time. Fold the egg whites into the chocolate mixture. Chill for 20–30 minutes until beginning to set.

Use some of the mousse to sandwich the 3 layers of meringue together, then cover the top and sides of the meringue layers with the remaining mousse. Cover the top and sides with the crushed meringue and dust the whole thing lightly with icing sugar and cocoa powder.

Chill for 4–24 hours, before serving.

Tiramisu in Chocolate Cups

There are a myriad recipes for tiramisu, but this one was inspired by a visit to *The Cipriani Hotel* in Venice where it is served in chocolate cups decorated with chocolate gondolas.

MAKES 6
225g/8oz plain chocolate, melted
250g/8½oz Mascarpone cheese
1 egg, separated
2 tbsp single cream
2 tsp caster sugar
few drops of natural vanilla essence
5 tbsp strong black coffee
2 tbsp coffee liqueur or brandy
6 sponge fingers
6 pairs of Amaretti biscuits
250ml/8fl oz double cream
1 tbsp cocoa powder

Brush the insides of 6 large paper cases which have a diameter of about 7.5–10cm/3–4in and are about 2.5cm/1in deep with an even layer of the melted chocolate and set them on a tray.

Chill for 15 minutes, then repeat the process and chill again for at least 15 minutes until hard.

When quite hard, carefully peel away the paper, leaving 6 chocolate cups.

Beat the Mascarpone with the egg yolk, single cream, 1 teaspoon of the

Tiramisu in Chocolate Cups and Trio of Chocolate Mousses

sugar and a few drops of vanilla essence until smooth.

In a small bowl, combine the coffee with the liqueur. Break the sponge fingers in half and dip each piece in the coffee mixture. Place 2 pieces in each chocolate cup and spread the Mascarpone mixture over the tops.

Break up the Amaretti biscuit pairs coarsely and dip the pieces in the remaining coffee mixture. Remove with a slotted spoon and place them in each chocolate cup.

Whisk the egg white until stiff, then whisk in the remaining sugar. Whisk the cream lightly with a few more drops of vanilla essence, then fold in the egg white.

Using a piping bag fitted with a large star nozzle (No. 8), pipe a whirl of the cream on top of each chocolate cup and dust with the cocoa powder.

Chill for up to 8 hours before serving.

Trio of Chocolate Mousses

Layer the three mousses in any order you wish. If you have plenty of time and patience, you can lay the glasses at various angles in the fridge to produce a more decorative effect.

MAKES 6
85g/3oz plain chocolate
1 tbsp milk
6 eggs
45g/1½oz unsalted butter
3 tbsp liqueur of choice
85g/3oz milk chocolate
85g/3oz white chocolate

In a small bowl set over simmering water, melt the plain chocolate with the milk. Beat in 2 of the egg yolks, one-third of the butter and 1 tablespoon of liqueur. Mix until smooth.

Whisk the whites of the 2 eggs until stiff then fold them into the plain chocolate mixture. Divide this between 6 long-stem glasses and chill for at least 30 minutes.

Make a milk chocolate mousse in a similar way but omit the milk when melting the chocolate. Spoon this into the glasses and chill for 1 hour. Make a white chocolate mousse layer in a similar way to the milk chocolate mousse layer.

Chill for at least 4 hours before serving.

Variation: for dark chocolate mousse, melt only plain chocolate with 3 tablespoons of milk and proceed as above.

Le Nègre

This French chocolate cake has no flour in it and produces a fairly dense, moist cake with a 'fudgy' texture.

200g/7oz unsalted butter, diced
200g/7oz plain chocolate (the darker, the better), broken into pieces
200g/7oz caster sugar
4 eggs, separated
icing sugar, to dust
cocoa powder, to dust
crème fraîche or Greek yogurt, to serve
fresh fruit, to serve

Preheat the oven to 190C/375F/gas5. Grease a 24cm/9½in springform tin with some butter and line the base with baking parchment.

Melt the chocolate in a bain-marie, then add the butter and stir until melted. Remove from the heat.

Add half the sugar to the egg yolks and whisk until pale and thick. Stir in the chocolate butter until evenly combined.

Whisk the egg whites until stiff. Then whisk in the remaining sugar, a little at a time, until thick and glossy. Fold this into the chocolate mixture and transfer to the prepared tin.

Bake for 40 minutes. Then leave to cool.

When the tin is cool enough to handle, unmould and dust with icing sugar and cocoa powder. Serve either warm, cold or chilled, cut into thin wedges and accompanied by a generous dollop of crème fraîche and some fruit.

Chocolate Soufflés in Orange Jackets

There's a certain amount of practice required to get these just right, but practice makes perfect and they are an impressive sight!

MAKES 6
6 large oranges
3 tbsp cocoa powder, sifted
45g/1½oz caster sugar
whites of 3 eggs (135ml/4½fl oz)

Cut a very small slice from the stem end of each orange so that they will all sit stably.

Cut across each orange two-thirds of the way up from this cut base. Squeeze out the juice from the tops and measure out 4 tablespoons.

Carefully remove all the flesh from inside the bases of the orange to leave 6 'jackets'. Set them on a baking tray.

Preheat the oven to 190C/375F/gas5.

Place the cocoa, one-third of the sugar and the measured orange juice in a saucepan and heat gently until evenly combined.

Whisk the egg whites to soft peaks then whisk in the remaining sugar a little at a time. Fold about one-quarter of the egg whites into the warm chocolate mixture to loosen it and then return the mixture to the bulk of the egg whites and fold in.

Spoon the mixture into the prepared orange jackets and bake for about 12 minutes until risen, but still slightly wobbly when shaken. Serve at once.

Chocolate Ravioli with Cointreau Sauce

Sweet ravioli may sound peculiar but give it a try – it'll be a great talking point at the table!

SERVES 4

FOR THE PASTA
170g/6oz plain flour
3 tbsp cocoa powder
2 tbsp caster sugar
pinch of salt
3 eggs
2 tbsp vegetable oil

FOR THE FILLING
170g/6oz curd or ricotta cheese
*55g/2oz glacé fruits, finely
chopped*
2 tbsp caster sugar
30g/1oz ground almonds

FOR THE COINTREAU SAUCE
300ml/½pt milk
pared zest of 1 orange
2 egg yolks
4 tbsp caster sugar
1 tsp cornflour
1 tbsp Cointreau

Make the pasta: in a bowl, sift the dry ingredients together. Separate one of the eggs and work in the yolk together with the 2 whole eggs and the oil to make a soft dough. If the mixture does not bind together very easily, add a very little water. Knead thoroughly until smooth. Wrap in cling film and leave to rest for about 20 minutes.

Make the filling by beating all the ingredients together.

Make the sauce: warm the milk with a large strip of orange zest in it. Beat the egg yolks with half the sugar and the cornflour until smooth. Pour on the hot milk, return to the saucepan and cook, stirring continuously, over a gentle heat until thickened. Strain through a fine sieve.

Cut the remaining orange zest into julienne strips and blanch them in a pan of boiling water. Drain them and place in a saucepan with the remaining sugar. Barely cover with water, bring to the boil and simmer gently until syrupy. Leave to cool.

Cut the piece of pasta dough in half and pass one portion through the rollers of a pasta machine several times, until smooth and as thin as possible. Place this on a lightly floured surface and cut out a 46×17.5cm/18×7in rectangle. Repeat with the second piece of pasta.

Spoon 12 mounds of filling on the pasta at regular intervals, 6 each along 2 lines. Brush the area of pasta between the filling and the edges with the reserved egg white. Carefully set the second piece of pasta on top and, starting in the centre, press down between each portion of filling so that it is completely sealed in. Using a pastry wheel or sharp knife, cut the pasta into 12 squares centred on each pile of filling.

Bring a large pan of lightly salted water to a good rolling boil, add a dash of oil and cook the ravioli in it for 5 minutes. Drain and place on a clean kitchen towel.

Warm the sauce gently, stir in the Cointreau and whisk until frothy. Spoon some of the sauce into each of 4 warmed soup plates and arrange 3 ravioli in each. Decorate with some of the candied orange julienne strips and serve at once.

Chocolate Truffle Cake

The first chocolate truffle cake I ever tasted was at the Swiss Centre in London, and the taste has stayed with me ever since. There are innumerable recipes for this type of cake, but the combination of dark chocolate and cocoa gives mine a fantastic flavour.

FOR THE SPONGE
2 eggs
55g/2oz caster sugar
30g/1oz plain flour, sifted
1 tbsp cornflour, sifted
2 tbsp cocoa powder, sifted

FOR THE TRUFFLE LAYER
2 tbsp Amaretto
2 tbsp strong black coffee
*85g/3oz plain chocolate, broken
into pieces*
2 tbsp milk
*115g/4oz unsalted butter, softened,
plus more for greasing*
115g/4oz caster sugar
75g/2½oz cocoa powder, sifted
3 egg yolks
*200g/7oz crème fraîche or soured
cream*
*55g/2oz Amaretti biscuits,
coarsely crushed*
icing sugar, to dust
cocoa powder, to dust

Preheat the oven to 190C/375F/gas5. Grease a 22cm/8½in cake tin with butter and line the base with greaseproof paper.

First make the sponge: put the eggs and sugar in a big bowl over a saucepan of simmering water and whisk with a hand-held electric whisk until thick and foamy (the whisk should leave a thick trail in the mixture). Remove from the heat. Sift together the dry ingredients and fold them in.

Transfer to the prepared tin, level the surface and bake for 15–18 minutes, until risen and just firm to the touch. Allow to cool in the tin, then unmould on a wire tray.

Line the sides of a 20cm/8in spring form tin with baking parchment. Set the sponge layer in the base of the tin and sprinkle it with the Amaretto and coffee.

In a small pan, melt the chocolate with the milk and stir until smooth. Beat the butter and sugar until light and fluffy then beat in the cocoa, egg yolks and crème fraîche. Stir in the melted and cooled chocolate.

Spoon this truffle mixture on top of the sponge and level the surface. Sprinkle with the crushed Amaretti biscuits and chill for at least 4 hours, or preferably overnight.

Unmould, dust lightly with icing sugar and cocoa powder and serve cut into very thin wedges.

Chocolate Truffle Cake

Presents
and Petits Fours

Home-made truffles, tuiles and
florentines are amongst the delights that
make wonderful gifts – especially when
they are beautifully presented in pretty
boxes, bright foil or colourful paper.
Make sure you always use excellent
chocolate, which is rich in cocoa solids
for a truly voluptuous flavour.

Fruit Dippers

You can have fun dipping your own fruits in chocolate, but always ensure that the fruit is whole and dry and prepare them on the day of serving to prevent the chocolate discolouring.

SERVES 8
85g/3oz each white and plain chocolate, melted
8 large strawberries, with stalks if possible
8 Cape gooseberries, with their papery covering pulled back
8 cherries, with stalks if possible

Put the white and dark chocolate in separate bowls set over saucepans of simmering water and stir until melted.

Wipe the fruits and make sure that they are all dry with no broken skin.

Dip the bottom half of the strawberries in the melted white chocolate and leave to set on baking parchment.

Dip the Cape gooseberries in dark chocolate to coat them completely. Leave to set on baking parchment.

Swirl the remaining dark and white chocolate together and dip the cherries in that. Leave to set on baking parchment.

Previous pages
Fruit Dippers and Afternoon Tea Truffles

Afternoon Tea Truffles

The addition of a little tea to the mixture gives these truffles a delicate flavour, so try experimenting with different blends.

MAKES 24
225g/8oz plain chocolate, broken into pieces
85g/3oz unsalted butter, diced
3 tablespoons freshly brewed tea, such as Earl Grey or mango
1 egg yolk
30g/1oz cocoa powder, sifted
1 tbsp ground cinnamon

Put the chocolate pieces, butter and tea in a small bowl set over a saucepan of simmering water and stir until the chocolate and butter have melted and the mixture is smooth. Beat in the egg yolk and chill until set.

Mix together the cocoa powder and cinnamon and scatter this on a tray.

Spoon small amounts of the chocolate mixture on the tray and roll them until evenly coated in the cocoa mixture. Lightly and quickly shape into rough balls with your fingers and shake off excess cocoa.

Chill until firm. Serve in petit four cases, if wished.

Tartletinis

This clever mixture shapes itself as it cooks, so just drop it into the miniature patty or petit four tins and watch for yourself. To ensure that they stay crisp, put the cream and fruit filling in the tartletinis just before serving.

MAKES 12
30g/1oz unsalted butter, softened
30g/1oz ground almonds
30g/1oz caster sugar
1½ tsp cocoa powder, sifted
4 tbsp cream, whipped to stiff peaks
1 small ripe mango, peeled, stoned and diced, or 12–36 fresh berries, depending on size
12 tiny mint sprigs

Preheat the oven to 190C/375F/gas5 and place 12 petit four tins on a baking tray or use a miniature patty tin tray.

In a bowl, work the butter, almonds, sugar and cocoa powder together then divide the mixture between the tins.

Bake for 20 minutes. Remove from the oven and allow to cool for no more than 5 minutes before carefully removing from the tins. Allow to cool on a wire tray until completely cold.

When cold, pipe a tiny whirl of cream in each case and top with 3–4 pieces of diced mango or 1–3 berries, depending on size. Decorate with a sprig of mint to serve.

Baboushka Triangles

Filo pastry is a wonderful ingredient to work with as long as you get good quality pastry as this produces fine and delicate results when baked – others may become tough and brittle and spoil the result. Please make an effort to look for the long boxes most commonly sold in specialist delicatessens.

MAKES 18
30g/1oz unsalted butter, melted,
plus more for greasing
55g/2oz stoned dates, finely
chopped
55g/2oz ready-to-eat dried
apricots, finely chopped
30g/1oz pistachio nuts, finely
chopped
1 tbsp flower blossom honey
115g/4oz white chocolate, melted
1 tbsp vegetable oil
3 sheets of filo pastry, each about
30×18cm/12×7in
1 tbsp sesame seeds or poppy
seeds, for sprinkling

Preheat the oven to 190C/375F/gas5 and grease a baking tray with butter.

In a bowl, combine the dates, apricots, nuts, honey and 1 tablespoon of the butter.

In another bowl, mix the chocolate and oil together until smooth.

Keeping the sheets of filo under a damp cloth, work with one sheet at a time. Spread each sheet with one-third of the chocolate mixture and then cut it across its length into 6 strips.

Place about 1 teaspoonful of the fruit mixture just in from the base of each strip and then fold the bottom right-hand corner of the strip diagonally over the filling so that the bottom edge of the strip is now covering the left-hand edge of the pastry.

Continue folding up the strip in the same way to finish with a triangular parcel. Continue with the remaining pastry, chocolate and filling to make 18 parcels in all.

Brush them with the remaining butter and then sprinkle lightly with sesame or poppy seeds. Place on the prepared baking tray.

Cook the parcels for 7–8 minutes, until golden. Allow to cool on a wire tray and serve fresh.

Normandy Truffles

The Calvados in these truffles gives them a wonderful flavour, but brandy may be used instead.

MAKES ABOUT 20
200g/7oz best-quality milk or
plain chocolate, broken into
pieces
3 tbsp creme fraîche or soured
cream
2 tbsp granulated sugar
2 tbsp Calvados
3–4 tbsp finely grated chocolate,
for coating (optional)

Put the chocolate pieces in a small bowl set over a saucepan of simmering water and stir until melted.

Place the cream and sugar in a small saucepan and bring to the boil over a moderate heat, then stir this into the chocolate. Mix until smooth, then stir in the Calvados.

Chill the mixture for about 30 minutes, until workable. Then shape into small cylinders between the fingertips. Roll in grated chocolate, if using. Chill until required.

Note: if wished, dip in melted chocolate instead of coating in grated chocolate. Leave on baking parchment in a cool place to set.

Whirligigs

These slim crisp biscuits are made by rolling together a brown and a white biscuit mixture and then cutting this in thin slices to reveal an attractive spiral pattern.

MAKES ABOUT 50

FOR THE WHITE BISCUIT MIXTURE
85g/3oz plain flour
55g/2oz butter, softened, plus more for greasing
30g/1oz caster sugar
1 tbsp milk

FOR THE BROWN BISCUIT MIXTURE
75g/2½oz plain flour
15g/½oz cocoa powder
55g/2oz butter, softened
30g/1oz caster sugar, plus more to finish
1 tbsp milk, plus more to finish

Make the white biscuit mixture: sift the flour into a small bowl. Rub in the butter until the mixture resembles fine crumbs, then stir in the sugar. Mix to a firm dough with the milk. Wrap and chill.

Make the brown biscuit mixture in a similar way: first sifting the flour and cocoa powder together. Wrap and chill.

On a lightly floured surface, roll out the white mixture to an oblong about 25×18cm/10×7in. Trim the edges.

Roll the dark mixture to a similar size and trim the edges.

Lightly brush the white oblong with a little of the extra milk and press the brown one on top. Brush the top very lightly with a little more extra milk and then roll up tightly, starting at a long edge.

Brush the roll lightly with more extra milk and then roll the cylinder in the extra caster sugar until lightly coated. Chill for 30 minutes.

Preheat the oven to 180C/350F/gas4 and grease a baking tray with butter.

Cut the biscuit roll in thin slices and place these slices on the prepared baking tray.

Bake for 20 minutes until lightly golden. Allow to cool on a wire tray.

Fruit and Nut Rocks

Use good-quality glacé fruits to give the best flavour to these quick chocolate sweets.

MAKES ABOUT 12
30g/1oz pecan nuts, finely chopped
1 slice of candied pineapple (about 50g/1¾oz), finely chopped
1 large candied clementine (about 50g/1¾oz), finely chopped
85g/3oz white chocolate, melted
2 tsp apricot brandy or orange liqueur

Place the nuts in a small non-stick frying pan and dry-fry them over a moderate heat until golden. Leave to go cold.

In a bowl, combine the cold nuts with the remaining ingredients then divide the mixture between 12 petit four cases. Chill until set.

Whirligigs and Fruit and Nut Rocks

Hazelnut Pralines

If you happen to be a fan of 'Black Magic' chocolates, you'll know these well. They're my favourites in that selection, so I thought I'd make a whole lot.

MAKES ABOUT 20
1 tsp vegetable oil, plus more for greasing
100g/3½oz skinned hazelnuts
85g/3oz caster sugar
½ vanilla pod, split
55g/2oz plain chocolate

Preheat the oven to 190C/375F/gas5 and lightly grease a baking tray with some oil.

Roast the hazelnuts for 15–20 minutes until golden.

In a small heavy-based pan, dissolve the sugar in 2 tablespoons of water and add the half vanilla pod. Then cook gently to a light caramel colour. Remove the vanilla pod, add the hazelnuts and toss them quickly in the caramel. Immediately turn out on the prepared tray.

Using two oiled forks, group the nuts into clusters of 4 (3 in a triangular base and 1 on top). (If the caramel sets while working with the nuts, then place the tray over a gentle flame to melt it again.) Leave to set hard.

Put the chocolate in a small bowl set over a saucepan of simmering water and stir until melted. Stir in the teaspoon of oil and leave to cool slightly.

Dip each of the nut clusters into the chocolate, shake off the excess and leave to set hard on a piece of baking parchment.

Chocolate and Walnut Sablés

These rich shortbread-type mouthfuls, with a glazed walnut topping, make a perfect gift.

MAKES ABOUT 36
170g/6oz unsalted butter at room temperature, plus more for greasing
85g/3oz caster sugar
1 egg, separated
250g/8½oz plain flour, sifted
15g/½oz cocoa powder, sifted
salt
30g/1oz chocolate drops
about 36 walnut halves
1 tbsp granulated sugar

Preheat the oven to 190C/375F/gas5 and lightly grease 2–3 baking trays with butter.

In a large bowl, cream the butter and caster sugar until soft and pale then beat in the egg yolk. Divide the mixture into 2 equal portions and put them in separate bowls.

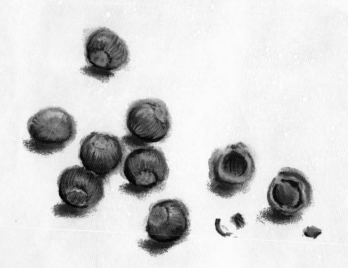

Into one portion mix 115g/4oz flour, the cocoa powder and a pinch of salt. Into the other mix the remaining flour, a pinch of salt and the chocolate drops. Work both mixtures to a firm dough.

Roll each mixture between 2 sheets of greaseproof paper to a thickness of about 1cm/½in. Stamp out as many 3.5cm/1½in rounds as possible, re-rolling the trimmings as necessary. Place the rounds on the prepared baking trays and press a walnut half in the top of each.

Whisk the egg white lightly with the granulated sugar and brush the surface of each biscuit with the mixture.

Bake for about 20 minutes until golden. Allow to cool on a wire tray. Store those not being used immediately in an airtight container.

Chocolate Fudge

The texture of home-made fudge can be sugary rather than creamy smooth, but the addition of butter and chocolate gives this one a wonderful texture. Omit the raisins if preferred.

MAKES 49 PIECES
55g/2oz raisins
about 5 tbsp dark rum
350g/12oz caster sugar
300ml/½pt milk
1 tbsp liquid glucose
115g/4oz butter, plus more for greasing
115g/4oz plain chocolate, melted

Put the raisins in a bowl and pour over just enough rum to cover them. Leave to macerate in a warm place for at least 1 hour, or even several days!

Place the sugar and milk in a large heavy-based saucepan and heat gently until the sugar is dissolved. Stir in the glucose and half the butter and bring to the boil, stirring all the time.

Cook the mixture slowly, stirring occasionally and brushing down the sides of the pan with water, for 20–30 minutes until the mixture is golden brown and thickened (about 108C/230F on a sugar thermometer, or when a little of the mixture goes firm when dropped on a well-chilled plate).

Remove from the heat and place the base of the pan in cold water to prevent further cooking. Beat thoroughly, adding the remaining butter, melted chocolate and well-drained raisins, until thick and creamy.

Transfer to a 19cm/7½in shallow square tin which has been greased with butter. Level the surface with a buttered knife and leave to set. When completely cold, cut into small squares.

Walnuts in Golden Shells

Toasted walnut halves are sandwiched together with chocolate and walnut paste and then dipped in light caramel to give the whole thing a thin brittle shell.

Make these on the day they are to be served and store them in an airtight container.

MAKES 20
40 walnut halves
30g/1oz walnut pieces
30g/1oz plain chocolate, melted and cooled
2 tsp egg white
vegetable oil, for greasing
170g/6oz granulated sugar

Preheat the oven to 190C/375F/gas5.

Place the walnut halves on one baking tray and the walnut pieces on another. Roast them for about 20 minutes until golden. Leave to cool.

Grind the walnut pieces finely in a coffee mill and mix with the chocolate and egg white to make a marzipan. Chill until firm.

Sandwich the walnut halves together in pairs with a little of the chocolate marzipan. Grease a baking tray lightly with oil.

In a small heavy-based pan, dissolve the sugar in 4 tablespoons of water over a gentle heat. Once the sugar has all dissolved, boil the syrup to a light golden colour. Remove from the heat and carefully tilt the pan.

One at a time, dip the walnuts in the caramel. Then lift them out with a fork, shake off the excess and place them on the oiled baking tray. Once all the walnuts are coated leave them to set hard.

Serve as petits fours. Store any not being used immediately in an airtight container. Best served on day of making.

Walnuts in Golden Shells

Mini Chocolate Meringue Tartlets

These tiny pastry cases contain a rich chocolate cream topped off with a swirl of meringue.

MAKES ABOUT 18

FOR THE PASTRY
85g/3oz plain flour
pinch of salt
55g/2oz unsalted butter, diced
1 tbsp caster sugar

FOR THE FILLING
1 egg, separated
55g/2oz plus 1 tbsp caster sugar
2 tbsp hot water
55g/2oz plain chocolate, melted
30g/1oz butter, melted
pinch of salt

First make the pastry: sift the flour and salt into a bowl. Then rub in the butter until the mixture resembles fine crumbs and stir in the sugar. Mix to a firm dough with 1½ teaspoons of cold water.

Roll out on a lightly floured surface and use to line about 18 miniature patty or petit four tins (1 tablespoon capacity), re-rolling trimmings as necessary. Prick the bases with a fork then chill for 20 minutes.

Preheat the oven to 190C/375F/gas5.

Bake the chilled pastry cases for 10 minutes then leave them to cool.

While they are cooling, leave the oven on and make the filling: whisk the egg yolk with the extra 1 tablespoon of sugar and 2 tablespoons of hot water until thick and foamy. Stir in the melted chocolate and butter and use the mixture to fill the pastry cases.

Return to the oven for about 5 minutes until the filling is lightly set. Remove the tartlets from the oven and turn it to its hottest setting.

Whisk the egg white with a pinch of salt until stiff then whisk in the remaining sugar, a little at a time, until the mixture is thick and glossy.

Fill a piping bag fitted with a small star nozzle (D8) with this meringue mixture and pipe a small circle of meringue on each tartlet.

Return them to the oven for 3–4 minutes, until the meringue is tinged an even golden brown.

Allow the tartlets to cool in their tins and eat fresh.

Mini Chocolate Meringue Tartlets, Chocolate Moneybags and Mini Ice-cream Cornets

Chocolate Moneybags

These moneybags are great fun to make yet look highly professional, so impress your friends with ease.

MAKES 8
4 sponge fingers, broken into
small pieces
1 tbsp fruit liqueur
55g/2oz fromage frais
8 fresh cherries, stoned and
halved or 16 raspberries
about 285g/10oz (1 quantity)
Chocolate Modelling Paste (see
page 19)

In a bowl, combine the sponge fingers with the liqueur, fromage frais and fruit to make the filling.

Divide the modelling paste into 8 even-sized pieces and knead them one piece at a time until soft. (If wished, the paste may be warmed in the microwave on Medium for a second or two to make it more pliable).

Roll out one piece of the paste between 2 sheets of baking parchment until it is very thin. Then trim it into a 10cm/4in square.

Spoon about one-eighth of the filling into the centre of the chocolate square then bring the corners up over the filling and squeeze quite tightly together just below the top to make a purse shape. Then repeat the rolling, trimming and filling for each of the other seven pieces.

Chill until ready to serve.

Mini Ice-cream Cornets

If at first you don't succeed, try, try, try again! Keep this phrase in mind as you make these little cornets – they are tricky to make, so spread and cook only two at a time.

MAKES ABOUT 30
30g/1oz unsalted butter, softened
45g/1½oz icing sugar, sifted
2 tbsp plain flour, sifted
1 tbsp cocoa powder, sifted
white of 1 egg (8 tsp), lightly whisked
2 tbsp clear honey
about 150ml/¼pt ice-cream or sorbet of your choice

Preheat the oven to 180C/350F/gas4 and line 2–3 baking trays with baking parchment.

In a bowl, cream the butter and sugar together to a soft consistency. Then gradually mix in the flour and cocoa powder with the egg white and honey to give a smooth soft mixture.

Place 2 separate teaspoons of the mixture well apart on each baking tray. Spread each spoonful of the mixture very thinly to make a round which has a diameter of about 7.5cm/3in diameter.

Bake for 7–8 minutes. Then remove from the oven and, within seconds, loosen the biscuits from the paper and wrap each one around a pastry horn mould.

Place on a wire tray and leave to go cold and crisp. Remove the mould. Cook the rest of the mixture in the same way in batches and store the cornets in an airtight tin until required.

When ready to serve, fill each cornet with a tiny ball of ice-cream or sorbet.

Mini Meringue Nests

These tiny meringue nests can be made well in advance and stored in an airtight container. They should only be filled shortly before serving.

MAKES 20

FOR THE MERINGUE
whites of 2 eggs (5 tbsp)
125g/4½oz icing sugar, sifted
¼ tsp salt

FOR THE FILLING
55g/2oz plain chocolate, melted
1 egg, separated
2 tsp butter
1 tbsp natural yogurt

Preheat the oven to 120C/250F/gas½ and line a baking tray with baking parchment.

Place the ingredients for the meringue in a bowl over simmering water and whisk with a hand-held electric mixer for 7–8 minutes until fairly stiff. Remove from the heat and continue whisking for 3–5 minutes more, until the bowl is cool and the mixture is really thick.

Fill a piping bag fitted with a small star nozzle (D8) with the meringue mixture. Starting in the centre, pipe small rounds with a diameter no larger than 4cm/1½in over the prepared baking tray. Then pipe 2 circles of meringue on top of the edge of each round, one on top of the other to form the nests. Once confident, this can all be done in one continuous spiral movement!

Bake the meringue nests for 1 hour until dried out – the meringues will then lift easily from the paper. Leave to go quite cold then store in an airtight container.

Just before serving, make the filling: in a bowl, beat together the chocolate, egg yolk and butter until smooth then fold in the yogurt.

Whisk the egg white until stiff and then fold this into the chocolate mixture. Spoon into the meringue nests to serve.

Toasted Hazelnut Clusters

These quick petits fours, consisting of toasted hazelnuts topped with a rich chocolate cream piped in a rosette, are easy to make and delicious with black coffee.

MAKES 16
48 whole hazelnuts
125ml/4fl oz double cream
115g/4oz plain chocolate, broken into pieces
1 tbsp dark rum or liqueur of your choice

Preheat the oven to 200C/400F/gas6.

Scatter the nuts on a baking tray and roast them for 15–20 minutes until golden. Leave to cool a little, then rub the nuts between your palms to remove the skins. Place 3 in each of 16 petit four cases.

Bring the cream just to the boil, then remove from the heat and stir in the chocolate until melted. Stir in the rum and then chill until firm.

Beat the firm chocolate mixture until it is soft and smooth. Then fill a piping bag fitted with a medium star nozzle with it and pipe a whirl of chocolate mixture on top of each cluster of hazelnuts. Chill until required.

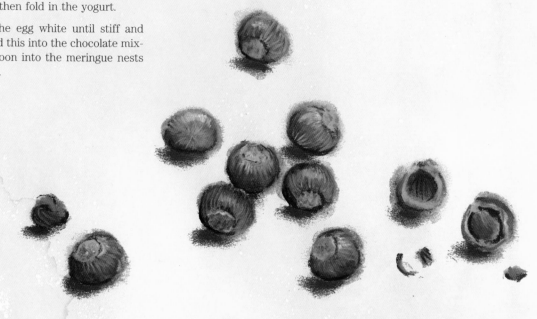

Chocolate Macaroons

These tiny macaroons will keep well in an airtight container. If preferred, they may also be sandwiched together in pairs with whipped cream.

MAKES 16
85g/3oz icing sugar
45g/1½oz ground almonds
2 tsp cocoa powder
white of 1 egg
pinch of salt
1½ tsp granulated sugar
1 tbsp flaked almonds, crushed

Preheat the oven to 180C/350F/gas4 and line a baking tray with a sheet of rice paper.

Sift the icing sugar, ground almonds and cocoa powder together into a bowl.

Whisk the egg white with a pinch of salt until it forms soft peaks then whisk in the granulated sugar. Fold in the sifted ingredients until evenly mixed.

Spoon or pipe 16 small dots evenly spaced on the piece of rice paper. Sprinkle with the crushed almonds and leave at room temperature for 15 minutes.

Bake for 20 minutes. Leave to go cold on the tray, then neaten the edges of each macaroon by trimming off excess rice paper.

Florentines

I know there are plenty of different sorts of commercially made florentines available in presentation boxes, but there's nothing like home-made.

MAKES 24
45g/1½oz butter
55g/2oz caster sugar
4 tbsp double cream
30g/1oz each pistachio nuts,
flaked almonds and walnut
pieces, coarsely chopped
30g/1oz glacé cherries, cut into
eighths
30g/1oz cut mixed peel
2 tbsp plain flour
55g/2oz plain or milk chocolate,
melted
55g/2oz white chocolate, melted

Preheat the oven to 180C/350F/gas4 and line 2–3 baking trays with baking parchment.

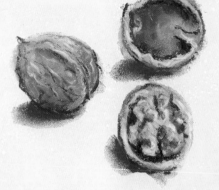

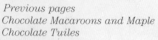

Previous pages
Chocolate Macaroons and Maple
Chocolate Tuiles

Place the butter, sugar and cream in a saucepan and heat gently until the butter melts. Bring just to the boil, stirring, then remove from the heat and stir in the nuts, fruit and flour and mix well until evenly combined.

Drop small spoonfuls of the mixture well apart on the prepared baking sheets. Bake for 15–20 minutes until golden.

If preferred, while they are still warm from the oven use a pastry cutter to pull in the edges of each florentine to make a neat shape. Leave to go quite cold, then lift off the paper.

Spread the flat side of half of the florentines with melted plain or milk chocolate and do the same to the rest with white chocolate. Leave to set.

Store those not being used immediately in an airtight container.

Maple Chocolate Tuiles

You'll most probably get into the swing of making these about half-way through the batch, so don't attempt to put more than four on each baking tray. Handle them carefully once baked, as they are delicate and quite brittle. Store very carefully in an airtight container.

MAKES ABOUT 30
55g/2oz unsalted butter
55g/2oz caster sugar
55g/2oz maple syrup or golden syrup
4 tbsp plain flour
1 tbsp cocoa powder
½ tsp ground cinnamon

Preheat the oven to 180C/350F/gas4 and line 2–3 baking trays with baking parchment or use non-stick trays.

Place the butter, sugar and syrup in a saucepan and heat gently until the butter has melted. Mix thoroughly and remove from the heat.

Sift the dry ingredients together and then beat them into the syrup mixture.

Spoon teaspoonfuls of the mixture well apart on the prepared trays and bake for about 10 minutes until bubbly and set.

Leave to cool on the paper for about a minute. Then lift off and curl around a rolling pin to mould into tuile shapes. Leave to go cold and crisp.

Store in an airtight tin.

Index